# rspb

# What's that
# BUTTERFLY?

# What's that
# BUTTERFLY?

## Tom Jackson

DK

**DK LONDON**
**Senior Editor** Peter Frances
**Editor** Lili Bryant
**Project Art Editor** Francis Wong
**Pre-production Producer**
Adam Stoneham
**Producer** Linda Dare
**Jacket Designer** Mark Cavanagh
**Jacket Design Development**
**Manager** Sophia MTT
**Managing Editor** Angeles Gavira Guerrero
**Managing Art Editor** Michelle Baxter
**Publisher** Sarah Larter
**Art director** Philip Ormerod
**Associate Publishing Director**
Liz Wheeler
**Publishing Director** Jonathan Metcalf

**DK DELHI**
**Senior Editor** Anita Kakar
**Editors** Susmita Dey, Himani Khatreja
**Art Editors** Sanjay Chauhan,
Divya P R, Vaibhav Rastogi
**DTP Designers** Sachin Gupta,
Nand Kishor Acharya
**Senior DTP Designer** Jagtar Singh
**Picture Researcher** Sumedha Chopra
**Managing Editor** Rohan Sinha
**Deputy Managing Art Editor**
Sudakshina Basu
**Pre-production Manager** Balwant Singh
**Production Manager** Pankaj Sharma

First published in Great Britain in 2014 by
Dorling Kindersley Limited,
80 Strand, London, WC2R 0RL
A Penguin Random House Company

2 4 6 8 10 9 7 5 3
009 – 192569 – Mar/2014

Copyright © 2016
Dorling Kindersley Limited

A CIP catalogue record for this book
is available from the British Library

ISBN 978-1-4093-4505-3

Printed and bound in China

A WORLD OF IDEAS:
SEE ALL THERE IS TO KNOW

www.dk.com

## ABOUT THE AUTHOR

**Tom Jackson** is a science
writer based in the UK.
He began his career as a
conservation worker and
zoologist, surveying the
jungles of Vietnam,
capturing buffaloes in
Zimbabwe, and working
in UK zoos. He has written
over 100 books on science,
technology, and nature,
and contributed to many
more. Tom lives in Bristol,
England. His earlier books
include *Help Your Kids
with Science* (with Carol
Vordeman), *Spot the
Bug*, and *DK Eyewitness
Books: Science, Animal*,
and *Endangered Animal*.

# Contents

Introduction ................................................................ 6

Identifying Butterflies and Moths .................................. 8

BUTTERFLY AND MOTH PROFILES     15

1 WHITE BUTTERFLIES AND MOTHS     16

2 GREEN BUTTERFLIES AND MOTHS     22

3 YELLOW BUTTERFLIES AND MOTHS     28

4 ORANGE BUTTERFLIES AND MOTHS     34

5 BROWN BUTTERFLIES AND MOTHS     48

6 GREY BUTTERFLIES AND MOTHS     76

7 BLACK BUTTERFLIES AND MOTHS     82

8 RED BUTTERFLIES AND MOTHS     90

9 PURPLE AND BLUE BUTTERFLIES AND MOTHS     96

BUTTERFLY GALLERY     104

MOTH GALLERY     110

Scientific Names .......................................................... 116

Glossary ...................................................................... 120

Index .......................................................................... 123

Acknowledgments ...................................................... 126

# Introduction

Butterflies are among the most colourful and conspicuous of insects, and it is always a pleasure to see them fluttering around a sunlit garden or dappled glade. Their moth cousins are the other side of the same coin. They have fewer fans, perhaps because they appear as night-time intruders rather than welcome visitors, but nevertheless, when seen close up, moths show off just as much delicate beauty as any butterfly. This book will help you identify butterflies and some day-flying moths, all species of which are arranged by their dominant colour and then by size. Even if you get just a passing glimpse of a butterfly or moth, you can turn to the relevant chapter and browse through for the best match. The book also includes information on how to get a longer, clearer look at these insects, which will reveal the intricacies of their amazing bodies. Whether you go looking for butterflies and moths or simply enjoy those that come to visit you, this book has all you need to get to know them better.

Tom Jackson

# Butterfly or Moth?

Although there is no clear scientific distinction between butterflies and moths, butterflies are generally colourful day-flyers, while moths are drab and nocturnal – but there are many exceptions.

### Butterflies

Generally, butterflies have clubbed antennae and smooth, slender bodies, while moths have tapered or feathered antennae and hairy, robust bodies. On the wing, butterflies look similar to moths. At rest, however, butterflies fold their wings together and hold them upright, above the body like a sail. The back of the forewing simply lies on top of the front of the hindwing.

Colourful wing pattern

Clubbed antennae

Large, rounded wings

**PAINTED LADY (RESTING POSITION)**

Hindwing connected to forewing by flap

Expanded hindwing base

Scale-covered wings

**PAINTED LADY (ON THE WING)**

## Moths

Most moths fly at night, but the ones that fly during the day outnumber the butterflies. When resting, moths hold their wings out sideways, either flat like an aircraft or angled into a tent shape. A moth's hindwing has bristles that connect to hooks on the forewing, holding the pair together.

Tapered antennae

**GARDEN CARPET (RESTING POSITION)**

Hairy body

Narrow wings

**GARDEN CARPET (ON THE WING)**

## Skippers

Members of a group of butterflies, skippers have some features in common with moths. Like other butterflies, skippers make short flights, or skips, during the day, but they share the drab colours of moths. Their resting posture is also a hybrid of the two types: hindwings are held flat, while forewings are elevated above the body.

Hooked antennae

Forewing held diagonally

Drab, hairy body

Hindwing held flat

**LULWORTH SKIPPER**

# Anatomy

Butterflies and moths make up the Lepidoptera order of insects, with around 175,000 species found all over the world, barring Antarctica. All members of this order have wings, six legs, and a body organized into a head, thorax, and abdomen. The eyes, mouth, and antennae are found on the head. The thorax bears the wings and legs, and the abdomen houses the digestive and reproductive systems.

Forewing

## Wings

Butterflies and moths have two pairs of wings – forewings and hindwings – with a combined surface area several times bigger than that of the body. Having large wings does not make them powerful fliers, and most Lepidopterans are only capable of short, frantic flights. The forewing and hindwing move together in flight. Most of the thrust comes from the forewings, while the hindwings are used for steering. The colours and patterns on the wings' undersides are usually more subdued than on the upperside.

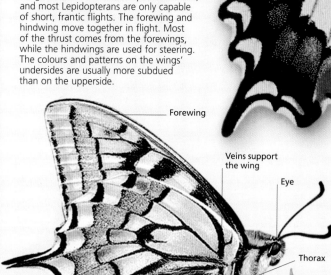

Forewing

Veins support the wing

Eye

Thorax

Leg

**SWALLOWTAIL (UNDERSIDE)**

Antenna

Leading edge

Head

Trailing edge

Abdomen

Scalloped margin

Hindwing

Tail streamer

**SWALLOWTAIL (UPPERSIDE)**

## Scales

Lepidoptera means "scale wings", and almost all species – those that do not have see-through wings – have wings covered in many thousands of tiny, flat scales. Wing scales are responsible for the vibrant colours and patterns; some scales are pigmented, while others reflect light in such a way that they create shimmering effects. Wing scales are fragile and fall away easily if the insect is handled roughly. There are also hair-like scales on other parts of the body.

# Identification

The differences between one species of butterfly or moth and another can be subtle. Most have very complex patterns made up of many colours and features, and it is common for members of a single species to be very varied in appearance.

## Markings and patterns

Most moths and butterflies are described by their colours, but the features on their wings are also crucial for identification. These features include various markings and patterns. Every species will have a unique combination of these.

Sooty brown background colour

**GROUND COLOUR**

Eye-like marking

**EYESPOTS**

Distinctive forewing tip

**WING TIPS**

Silvery markings (pearls)

**PEARLS**

Solid circles that may be ringed

**SPOTS**

Crescent-shaped markings (scallops)

Long tail streamer

**SCALLOPS AND TAILS**

Blotches of colour on pale background

**MARBLING**

Dark coloured supporting veins

**VEINS**

Thick stripe across wing

**BANDS**

Shimmering, metallic hues

**IRIDESCENCE**

Thin line along wing

**HAIRSTREAK**

Irregular wing margin

**JAGGED WING**

## Sex

Members of one species of moth or butterfly can look quite different from each other. This difference is most common between the sexes, with males being brighter and more colourful than the females to attract mates, as in the case of the Emperor Moth.

Antennae are more feathery than in female

Lighter colouring than male

**FEMALE**

**MALE**

## Brood

The colour of some species varies according to the time of year in which they hatch. The first brood, also known as the spring brood, can be strikingly different from the the second, summer, brood as in the case of the Map.

Orange-brown, with black spots

Black, with white markings

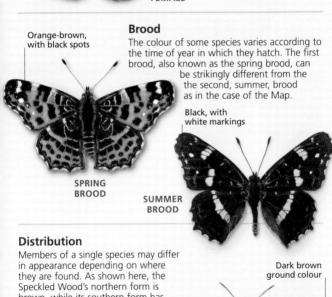

**SPRING BROOD**

**SUMMER BROOD**

## Distribution

Members of a single species may differ in appearance depending on where they are found. As shown here, the Speckled Wood's northern form is brown, while its southern form has a more orange ground colour.

Dark brown ground colour

Orange and brown ground colour

**NORTHERN FORM**

**SOUTHERN FORM**

# Spotting Butterflies

On sunny days, butterflies are a common sight in gardens and the countryside. However, it helps to know where to look to find the rarer species. Wherever you look, butterfly spotting will require patience.

### Where to look

The best time to observe a butterfly is when it feeds. Butterflies are liquid feeders and visit flowers and ripe fruit to drink nectar and juice. They like flowers such as buddleia, verbena, lavender, scabious, and thistle.

**LAVENDER**

**Puddles**
Butterflies need to drink water and often crowd around puddles, or even sip from damp sand. This is called puddling.

**Sunny spots**
In colder areas, butterflies need to warm up before they can fly. They can be seen basking, with wings stretched out, on large leaves and tree trunks.

**Habitats**
Sunny gardens and meadows are good places to spot moths and butterflies, but these insects are also common along hedgerows, in woodland glades, and on moorlands.

**GARDEN**      **WOODLAND GLADE**

### Equipment for the field

Handling butterflies and moths can damage their wings, so taking photographs of them is a good way to identify tricky species that do not stay still for long. A lamp or torch creates a "light trap" for attracting night-flying species.

**DIGITAL CAMERA**

**OIL LAMP**

# BUTTERFLY AND MOTH PROFILES

The species profiled in this book are mostly seen during the day. Moths and butterflies are grouped into sections on the basis of colour. Within each chapter, the species are arranged by wingspan – the distance between wing tips – from smallest to largest. While the smallest would fit on a thumbnail, the largest species can fill a palm.

**16** WHITE BUTTERFLIES AND MOTHS
**22** GREEN BUTTERFLIES AND MOTHS
**28** YELLOW BUTTERFLIES AND MOTHS
**34** ORANGE BUTTERFLIES AND MOTHS
**48** BROWN BUTTERFLIES AND MOTHS
**76** GREY BUTTERFLIES AND MOTHS
**82** BLACK BUTTERFLIES AND MOTHS
**90** RED BUTTERFLIES AND MOTHS
**96** PURPLE AND BLUE BUTTERFLIES
AND MOTHS

## Symbols

↔ Wingspan  ● Upperside
♂ Male  ● Underside
♀ Female

# 1 WHITE BUTTERFLIES AND MOTHS

White butterflies and moths are often easy to spot because they stand out among foliage. Not all, however, are pure white. Some have wings dominated by white or pale cream, although conspicuous markings of other colours can also be present.

## BLUE-BORDERED CARPET

Moth seen in summer, mostly in marshy areas but also in gardens and woodland, especially near ponds. As its name suggests, this species has a blue-grey fringe on the forewing's trailing edge. It occurs in two forms – the southern form has brown spots, which become a solid bar in the northern form.

Brown spots on southern form

Blue-grey fringe on forewing

↔ 2.2–2.8 cm

## SILVER-GROUND CARPET

Moth seen both by day and night, found in ferns, gardens, and heathland, as well as in thickets, bushes, and woodland edges. The triangular wings are silver-white with a jagged band of brown and black running across them.

Silver-white ground colour

Brown and black band

Triangular wing

↔ 2.9–3.3 cm

## BLACK-VEINED MOTH

Day-flying moth, widespread in Europe but restricted to a part of southeastern Britain. Unlike white butterflies, this moth holds its wings in a flat triangle when resting and the veins are also darker, especially on the upperside.

White or
pale cream
ground colour

Black veins

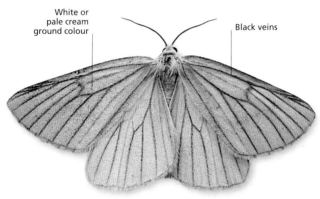

✛ 3.8–4.8 cm

## ORANGE-TIP

Butterfly mostly seen in spring. Males (shown here) have distinctive orange tips to forewings, while females have green-grey tips. The underside in both sexes has a marbled pattern of green blotches on a white background.

Orange tip
on forewing

Dark spot
on forewing

Green marbling

✛ 4–5.2 cm

»

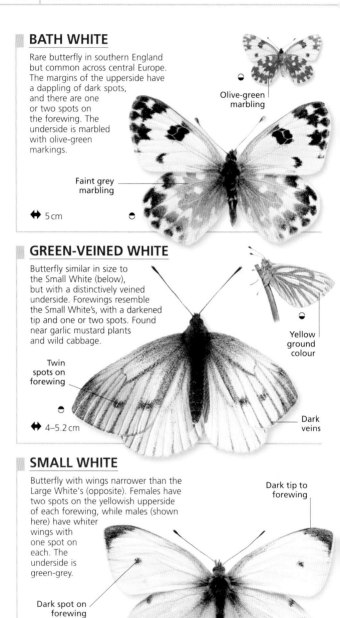

## BATH WHITE

Rare butterfly in southern England but common across central Europe. The margins of the upperside have a dappling of dark spots, and there are one or two spots on the forewing. The underside is marbled with olive-green markings.

Olive-green marbling

Faint grey marbling

↔ 5 cm

## GREEN-VEINED WHITE

Butterfly similar in size to the Small White (below), but with a distinctively veined underside. Forewings resemble the Small White's, with a darkened tip and one or two spots. Found near garlic mustard plants and wild cabbage.

Yellow ground colour

Twin spots on forewing

↔ 4–5.2 cm

Dark veins

## SMALL WHITE

Butterfly with wings narrower than the Large White's (opposite). Females have two spots on the yellowish upperside of each forewing, while males (shown here) have whiter wings with one spot on each. The underside is green-grey.

Dark tip to forewing

Dark spot on forewing

↔ 3.8–5.7 cm

# WOOD WHITE

Butterfly with weak flight, seen occasionally in southern Britain and Ireland. It has a white upperside with a smudge of grey at the tip of each forewing. The streaky underside is a yellow-grey.

Grey streaks

Broad, rounded hindwing

Slender body

↔ 6 cm

# LARGE WHITE

Strong-flying butterfly, seen from March to October. The forewings are white with a dark tip; females also have two dark spots (male shown here). On the underside, the hindwing is yellow-tinged and the forewing has two dark spots in both sexes.

Yellow-grey ground colour

Dark tip on forewing

Greyish black edge

↔ 6 cm

Creamy ground colour

# 2 GREEN BUTTERFLIES AND MOTHS

Green is an uncommon colour for butterflies and moths, with only a few being green all over. Some may only have a green underside, providing a degree of camouflage when resting on leaves. Other species have a metallic green sheen.

## CISTUS FORESTER

Similar to but smaller than the Forester (opposite), with a bluer tinge to its metallic green wings. Found in central and southern areas of Britain, this day-flying moth is seen mainly on chalky grasslands.

Feathery antennae of male

Metallic green forewing

✦ 2.3–2.5 cm

## GREEN CARPET

Widespread moth, a vibrant mottled green when newly emerged, fading to a yellow-grey as it ages. The Green Carpet flies from May to September, generally at dusk, but it is often disturbed from plants during the day.

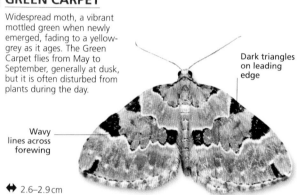

Dark triangles on leading edge

Wavy lines across forewing

✦ 2.6–2.9 cm

## GREEN HAIRSTREAK

Butterfly most often observed in spring and early summer. The commonly seen underside is yellow-green. A dashed white line runs along both wings. The upperside is a dark, uniform brown, but this butterfly is rarely seen in flight.

Scalloped edge

Clear, broken white line on hindwing

✦ 2.7–3.4 cm

## FORESTER

Distinctive, small moth with metallic green wings. It flies by day and is seen in damp grasslands, woodland clearings, and sandy heaths throughout summer.

Strongly feathered antennae of male

Blackish hindwing

↔ 2.5–3 cm

## EASTERN DAPPLED WHITE

A migrant from France and southern Europe that is seen only rarely in the British Isles. The upside is white with a dark, dappled tip. The underwing is marbled with olive-green spots.

Black spot on forewing

Olive-green marbling

↔ 3.5 cm

## BRIMSTONE

One of the first butterflies to be seen in spring, the Brimstone flies until late summer, with distinctively hooked forewings. While the upside is pale yellow, the leaf-green veined underside is more likely to be seen as it rests.

Angular hindwing

Orange spot on hindwing

↔ 6–7.4 cm

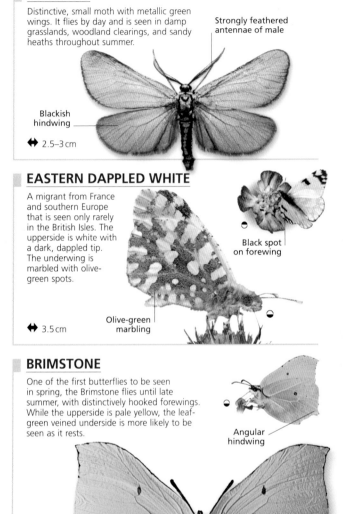

# Life Cycle

A butterfly or moth's winged form is the final and short-lived stage of a complex life cycle. The insect spends most of its life in a wingless larval form before undergoing the transformation into an adult.

A butterfly or moth hatches out of an egg as a caterpillar – a worm-like animal that does nothing but eat and grow. Once it is big enough, the caterpillar's body shuts down and is transformed into the flying adult in a process called complete metamorphosis.

### Stages of growth

Having different larval and adult stages ensures that the young and adults do not compete for food and space. Caterpillars eat fruit and leaves, while adults sip nectar. To metamorphose, the insect enters an inactive phase, during which it is encased in a structure called a chrysalis.

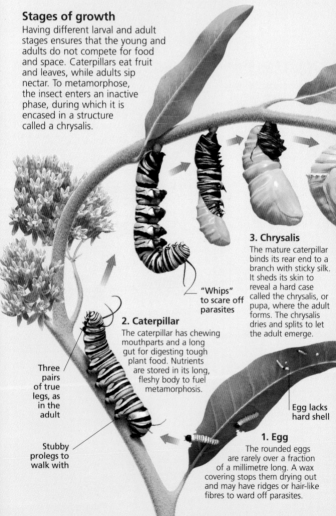

**3. Chrysalis**
The mature caterpillar binds its rear end to a branch with sticky silk. It sheds its skin to reveal a hard case called the chrysalis, or pupa, where the adult forms. The chrysalis dries and splits to let the adult emerge.

"Whips" to scare off parasites

**2. Caterpillar**
The caterpillar has chewing mouthparts and a long gut for digesting tough plant food. Nutrients are stored in its long, fleshy body to fuel metamorphosis.

Three pairs of true legs, as in the adult

Egg lacks hard shell

**1. Egg**
The rounded eggs are rarely over a fraction of a millimetre long. A wax covering stops them drying out and may have ridges or hair-like fibres to ward off parasites.

Stubby prolegs to walk with

### 4. Adult butterfly

After emerging, the adult rests for a few hours for its body to harden. As it will survive for only a few days or weeks, its main role is to find a mate and produce the next generation.

Antennae detect mates by their smell

Colourful wings attract mates

Sex organs lie in abdomen

Wings are folded tightly against body inside hard pupal case

Adult emerges

Pupal case is left behind

Blood is pumped into wings to spread them out

### Mating and egg laying

After mating, the male leaves to find another mate, while the female looks for a plant – one that will provide the right food for the hatched caterpillars – on which to lay her eggs. The eggs lie dormant in winter, and the caterpillars hatch in spring.

# 3 YELLOW BUTTERFLIES AND MOTHS

Yellow butterflies and moths are frequently related to white ones. Together, they form the Pieridae family. It is even suggested that the word "butterfly" is derived from the butter yellows of some common species.

## BARRED YELLOW

Small woodland moth seen in June and July. The Barred Yellow can be almost brown in northern regions and brighter in the south. It has a wide, dark brown stripe across its forewings.

Bright yellow ground colour

Brown V-shaped band on forewing

↔ 2.5–3 cm

## SPECKLED YELLOW

Yellow moth with grey-brown speckles on the upperside. It can be seen from April to July, and is generally more common in the warmer southern parts of its range.

Dark brown blotches

Dark tip

↔ 2.8–3 cm

## YELLOW SHELL

Small moth with fine wing lines that are alternately light and dark. It is darker in the north of its range. Found in a wide variety of habitats, it is seen mostly around dusk but can be found resting on shrubs during the day.

Dark and light wavy lines on forewing

Yellow ground colour

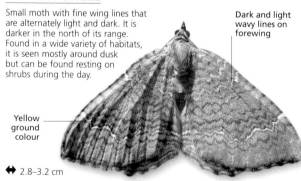

↔ 2.8–3.2 cm

## THE SPINACH

Yellow moth with an unusual resting position. It holds its forewings at right angles to its body, almost completely covering its hindwings. Wavy, dark brown lines give the wings the appearance of wood grain.

Chequered wing fringe

Wavy, dark brown lines

↔ 3.3–3.8 cm

## BRIMSTONE MOTH

Day- and night-flying moth with bright yellow triangular wings. It has reddish brown blotches along the leading edges of its forewings. It can be found in woodland, scrub, and grassland habitats.

Reddish brown mark on forewing

Unmarked hindwing

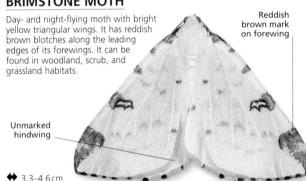

↔ 3.3–4.6 cm

## CLOUDED BUFF

Summer moth seen in meadows, heathland, chalk woodland, and woodland clearings. The male has pink fringes on white hindwings. The females are smaller and more orange, with black veins. The sexes are sometimes mistaken for members of different species.

♀

Orange-red forewing

♂

Bright yellow forewing

↔ 3.5–5 cm

»

## HORNET MOTH

Moth with transparent wings and a yellow-and-black striped body. Often mistaken for a giant wasp, it uses this disguise to scare predators. Nevertheless, it is very rarely seen and is always found close to poplar trees, where it lays its eggs.

Thickened antennae

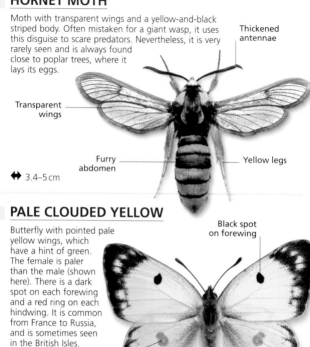

Transparent wings

Furry abdomen

Yellow legs

↔ 3.4–5 cm

## PALE CLOUDED YELLOW

Butterfly with pointed pale yellow wings, which have a hint of green. The female is paler than the male (shown here). There is a dark spot on each forewing and a red ring on each hindwing. It is common from France to Russia, and is sometimes seen in the British Isles.

Black spot on forewing

Red ring on hindwing

↔ 5 cm

## CLOUDED YELLOW

Fast-flying butterfly seen from May to October, sometimes in large numbers. The males (shown here) are golden yellow, but the females are closer to green. There is a dark spot on each forewing. Each hindwing has both a large and a small pale spot on the underside.

Dark spot on forewing

Broad, dark brown margin

↔ 5.2–6.2 cm

# SCARCE SWALLOWTAIL

Large butterfly similar to the Swallowtail (below)
but paler. Each hindwing ends in a tail-like extension
and bears an orange eyespot and crescent-shaped
blue fringing on the upperside. A rare visitor to
Britain, it is only seen in April and May.

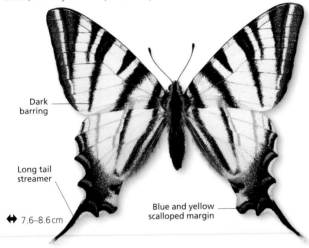

Dark barring

Long tail streamer

Blue and yellow scalloped margin

↔ 7.6–8.6 cm

# SWALLOWTAIL

One of the biggest butterflies of Europe, named
for the distinctive tail-like extensions on its hindwings.
The Swallowtail's upperside has a fringe of black,
with blue and red eyespots on each hindwing.
The underside is yellow with black stripes.

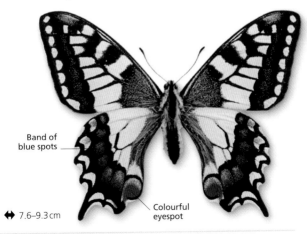

Band of blue spots

Colourful eyespot

↔ 7.6–9.3 cm

# 4 ORANGE BUTTERFLIES AND MOTHS

Orange butterflies and moths can have ground colour ranging from buff-orange to vibrant copper. These butterflies include many species of fritillary, a name derived from the Latin for "dice" and referring to the butterflies' chequered pattern.

## PURPLE-BORDERED GOLD

Tiny, day-flying moth, seen around fenland and damp heathland in early summer. Its wings have a feathery fringe, and their shape resembles that of a butterfly's. The orange wings are covered with distinctive pink spots and have a darker purple border.

Distinct purple border

Feathery fringe

↔ 1.8–2 cm

## DUKE OF BURGUNDY

One of the rarest butterflies. It is seen in late spring, sitting on grasses with its wings held flat. The upperside is brown with orange chequers and a fringe of white spots. The orange underside has a white band on the hindwings and dark spots on the forewings.

Orange-buff spots

Chequered fringe

↔ 3 cm

## SMALL COPPER

Often seen in large numbers, with male butterflies basking on stones to attract females. On the upperside, their copper forewings have brown spots and margins. The hindwings are mostly brown with a coppery fringe. The undersides are paler with black spots.

Black spots

Orange forewing

Orange band near margin

↔ 2.6–3.6 cm

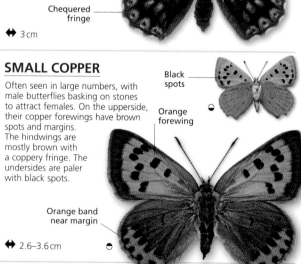

## ORANGE UNDERWING

Day-flying moth found in early spring. At rest, its orange hindwings are hidden by brown and white forewings, which also camouflage the moth as it perches on silver birch bark. As it flies, the hindwings create flashes of orange.

Light patches on brown forewing

Orange hindwing

↔ 3.5–3.9 cm

## NARROW-BORDERED BEE HAWK-MOTH

Day-flying moth that looks like a large bumble-bee, seen between April and July. A dark, narrow border runs along the outer edge of its transparent wings. The body is covered in golden hairs. These wear away with age to reveal dark bands.

Dark stripe around forewing

Golden hairs on body

↔ 4.1–4.6 cm

## GLANVILLE FRITILLARY

Orange and yellow bands

Summer-flying species, restricted to Channel Islands and Isle of Wight in Britain. The upperside is fringed with white. There are four or five black spots on a band of orange chequers on the hindwings. The underside is much paler, comprising curved orange and yellow bands.

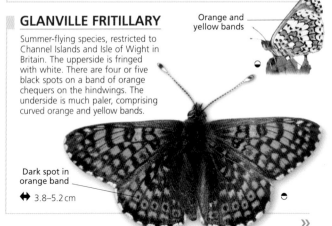

Dark spot in orange band

↔ 3.8–5.2 cm

»

# GATEKEEPER

Butterfly with rich orange upperside and wide brown wing margins. Twin dark eyespots with two white highlights appear near the tips of the forewings on both the upperside and underside. The Gatekeeper is often seen on flowers that grow in gateways and gaps in hedges.

Buff-yellow ground colour

Highlights on twin eyespot

Dark patch on forewing

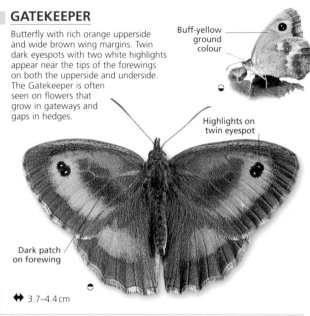

↔ 3.7–4.4 cm

# HEATH FRITILLARY

Butterfly with a mosaic effect on its orange upperside, which is crisscrossed with thick black lines. The underside is much paler, with a yellowish central band. This rare fritillary is seen between May and September in woodlands and on moors in parts of southeast and southwest England.

Yellowish central band

Network of black markings

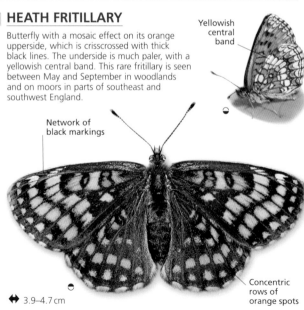

Concentric rows of orange spots

↔ 3.9–4.7 cm

## QUEEN OF SPAIN FRITILLARY

One of the fastest flying butterflies, with conspicuous black spots on its orange upperside. The underside of the forewing is similar, but the hindwing has large silvery spots. A rare migrant, this fritillary can be seen as early as February.

Marbled brown
hindwing

Orange
ground
colour

Angular
wing
margin

↔ 3.4–5.6 cm

## SMALL TORTOISESHELL

Colourful butterfly with a distinctive fringe of blue spots along the trailing edges of its upperside. Seen resting with its wings held flat, the Small Tortoiseshell is one of the most commonly seen butterflies across Europe, flying from March to October.

Smoky brown
ground colour

Yellow
and
black
markings

↔ 4.5–6.2 cm

Blue spots
along margin

»

## PEARL-BORDERED FRITILLARY

Fritillary with forewings considerably larger than hindwings. Pearl-like white spots fringe the underside of this butterfly's hindwing, and its deep orange upperside is covered with black spots. It is seen from late April to June and sometimes until August.

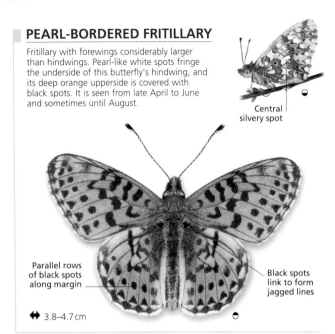

Central silvery spot

Parallel rows of black spots along margin

Black spots link to form jagged lines

↔ 3.8–4.7 cm

## MAP (SPRING BROOD)

Rare butterfly that produces two broods each year with strikingly different coloration. The spring brood has an orange upperside with chunky black markings and white spots near the tips. With its lilac ground colour and white bands, the underside resembles a map. The summer brood (p.86) is black.

Intricate pattern of white veins

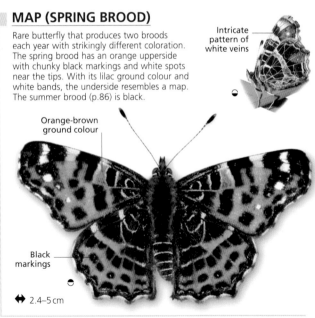

Orange-brown ground colour

Black markings

↔ 2.4–5 cm

## MARSH FRITILLARY

Butterfly with a highly chequered upperside and a paler pattern on the underside. Adult Marsh Fritillaries are seen from mid-May to June in marshy grasslands. Habitat loss has made this butterfly rare in recent years.

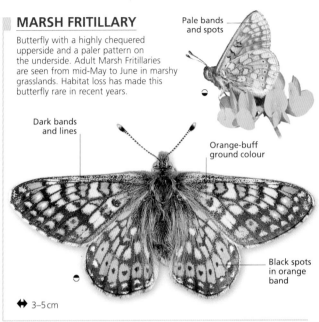

Pale bands and spots

Dark bands and lines

Orange-buff ground colour

Black spots in orange band

↔ 3–5 cm

## COMMA

Butterfly with distinctive ragged wing edges. It gets its name from the comma-shaped white mark on the underside of each hindwing. The orange upperside has chunky dark markings. The Comma flies from March to September.

Small white comma mark

Dark markings

Jagged wing margin

↔ 5–6.4 cm

》

# Feeding

The best time to see a butterfly or moth is when it flies from flower to flower, feeding on nectar. However, as a caterpillar it fuels itself in a very different way.

Adult butterflies or moths mostly drink sugary liquids – in the form of nectar and fruit juices – to power their energetic flights in search of mates. Caterpillars, however, are only concerned with growth. They devour vast quantities of food as they race to reach the right size for metamorphosis.

## Caterpillars

Most caterpillars eat plants – they chew holes in leaves, destroy roots, and burrow inside fruit. Clothes moth larvae eat the wool in clothes and carpets, and they even eat hair. Caterpillars use their robust mouthparts to slice and scrape off food and chew it to a pulp.

Claw-like legs

**Hungry caterpillar**
Plant food is not very nutritious, which is why caterpillars have to eat a lot of it. During their lifetime, they consume several thousand times their body weight in food, and can grow to around 1,000 times their hatching size.

"Hair" to defend against parasites

Body stores nutrients as fat

**Poisonous feast**
Many species, such as this Swallowtail caterpillar, eat poisonous plants. The toxins do not hurt them but are stored in their bodies. If a predator eats this caterpillar it will be sick and will learn to avoid eating more of them.

**Production line**
Silkworms are moth caterpillars that can only survive in silk factories and not in the wild. They are fed the leaves of mulberry bushes. The silk produced is collected from the caterpillar's cocoon.

## Liquid feeders
Adult butterflies or moths consume mostly liquids, as well as some pollen. They require liquids that are full of energy, and most consume sugar-rich foods such as nectar, fruit juices, and sap. However, a few drink the liquids oozing from rotting animals and dung.

Coiled proboscis

## Flower power
When a butterfly or moth drinks the nectar from flowers, its feet are dusted with pollen, which it transfers to other flowers it visits. This pollen fertilizes the ovaries of that flower and produces seeds.

## Proboscis
The mouthparts of an adult butterfly or moth consist of a drinking tube called a proboscis. When not being used, this is coiled up under the head.

## LARGE COPPER

Distinctive copper-coloured butterfly often seen near waterside vegetation, particularly in damp fenland habitats. The male butterfly's upperside is almost entirely a deep orange, apart from a dark margin and a dark spot on each forewing. The female's forewing has several spots, and the hindwing has solid brown blocks. The underside of both sexes is similar – silvery hindwings and orange forewings with black spots.

Black spot on hindwing

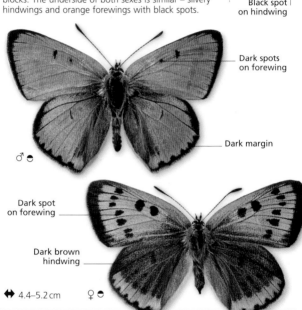

Dark spots on forewing

Dark margin

♂ ◑

Dark spot on forewing

Dark brown hindwing

↔ 4.4–5.2 cm    ♀ ◑

## PAINTED LADY

Migratory butterfly – spreading up from North Africa – with a distinctive orange and brown upperside. It has white spots on dark-tipped forewings. The hindwing underside is mottled brown. It is frequently seen with wings held flat at rest.

Salmon-pink forewing

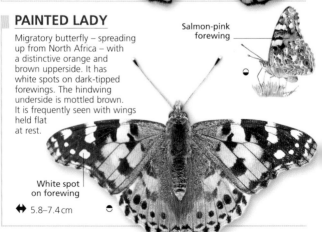

White spot on forewing

↔ 5.8–7.4 cm    ◑

# SILVER-WASHED FRITILLARY

Easy to differentiate from other large orange fritillaries by its pointed forewings and silver-streaked underside. This species is seen flying high in woodlands in summer and is easiest to spot in sunny clearings. It is most common in southern England and Wales.

Silvery band

Black spots

↔ 6.9–8 cm

# KENTISH GLORY

Large moth; males have orange hindwings while females are browner. Males (shown here) also have feathery antennae, unlike females. Seen in spring, males fly during the day, while females only emerge at dusk.

Brown and white marking on forewing

Feathery antenna

↔ 5.8–8.9 cm

»

## HIGH BROWN FRITILLARY

Butterfly distinguished from the more common Dark Green Fritillary (below) by orange-ringed pearls along the underside of the hindwing. It can be seen in summer among bracken and woodland shrubs. This butterfly is rare in the British Isles.

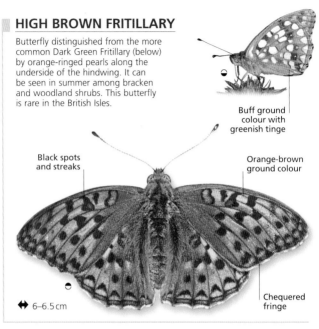

Buff ground colour with greenish tinge

Black spots and streaks

Orange-brown ground colour

Chequered fringe

↔ 6–6.5 cm

## DARK GREEN FRITILLARY

Widespread fritillary, with a distinctive green underside to its hindwings. A powerful flyer, it is a butterfly of open habitat and is often seen on flowers such as thistle and knapweed. Like most fritillaries, it has an orange upperside with dark spots.

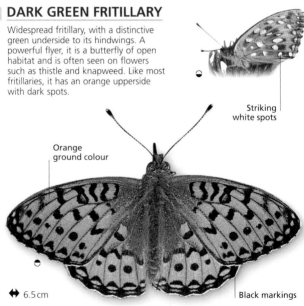

Striking white spots

Orange ground colour

Black markings

↔ 6.5 cm

## LARGE TORTOISESHELL

Larger, but less brightly coloured, butterfly than the Small Tortoiseshell (p.39). The upperside is mostly orange with a few dark spots on the forewing and faint blue crescents along the jagged trailing edge. It typically frequents branches of tall trees, making it hard to spot.

Series of jagged brown bands

Squarish black spots

Jagged wing edges

↔ 8 cm

## MONARCH

Large butterfly blown across from North America. The orange of the wings is darker on the upperside than the underside. It has black stripes and a distinctive dark margin studded with little white spots.

Network of black veins

Black body with white spots

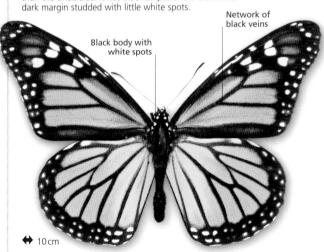

↔ 10 cm

# 5 BROWN BUTTERFLIES AND MOTHS

Their colour and patterning make brown butterflies and moths tricky to spot against tree bark, rocks, and soils. They include several hairstreak butterflies – named after the narrow white stripes on their wings – and some underwing butterflies.

## DIAMOND-BACK MOTH

Moth with very long, narrow wings, giving it an unusual appearance. It has an ungainly flying style, resembling that of a small fly. At rest, with its wings folded along its body, a row of tan-coloured diamond shapes can be seen where the two forewing edges meet. This moth is widespread from May to September and is especially common around cabbage fields.

Forward-pointing antennae

Buff-coloured band

Long, thin forewing

Wing tip fringed with long hairs

✥ 1.3–1.5 cm

## MINT MOTH

Tiny moth with rusty brown forewings that have a distinctive golden spot near the tip. There may be smaller yellow markings as well. A golden band runs across the dark brown hindwings. A widespread moth, it is seen around wild mint and thyme.

Thickened antennae

Distinct golden spot on forewing

✥ 1.8–2 cm

## SMALL BLUE (FEMALE)

Butterfly with a dark brown upperside, despite belonging
to the blue family. The underside, like that of the male
(p.98), is pale blue with dark spots ringed in white.
The Small Blue is seen throughout the summer. It
may perch on human skin to feed on sweat.

Sooty
brown
wings

White
fringe

↔ 1.8–2.7 cm

## GRIZZLED SKIPPER

Butterfly with a dark brown upperside peppered with white
spots. When perching, this skipper raises its wings to reveal a
paler brown underside, with the same large white markings.
It is seen on chalky hills and meadows in spring and summer
but is becoming rare.

White spots

Broken
white fringe

↔ 2.3–2.9 cm

Black body

»

## BEAUTIFUL YELLOW UNDERWING

Small, striking moth with hindwings that are yellow-tinged on the upperside. The forewings are red-brown, with wavy black and white stripes running across them. This moth feeds on heather, which is the best place to seek it out. It can be seen making quick flights across sunny moorlands in summer.

Red-brown forewing

Wavy white stripe

↔ 2–2.2 cm

## FIELD BINDWEED MOTH

Moth with white patches on the upperside of each wing. The rest of the upperside is an intricate collection of black, grey, and brown wavy lines. The white patches provide camouflage as it perches among the small white flowers of field bindweed, which is its preferred food source. It is also known as the Four-spotted moth.

Black, grey, and brown ground colour

White patch on forewing

↔ 2.2–2.5 cm

## CLOAKED MINOR

Slender antennae

Varied moth named for the way its forewings can be divided into a red-brown upper section and a paler lower half, making it look like it is wearing a cloak. The forewings may be a uniform straw colour or the cloak may be reduced to a thick band. It is found near sand dunes and on chalky hills. Females fly at night, while the males are seen from late afternoon onwards.

Narrow forewing

↔ 2.2–2.8 cm

## COMMON HEATH

Moth closely resembling the Latticed Heath (p.58) in its freckled pattern of brown spots, but it can be identified by the way it holds its wings at rest – in a flat, triangular shape. In some cases, the light and dark brown patches merge into branching bands that cross the whole wing, but they may also be less distinct blotches.

Feathery antennae in males

Light and dark brown patches

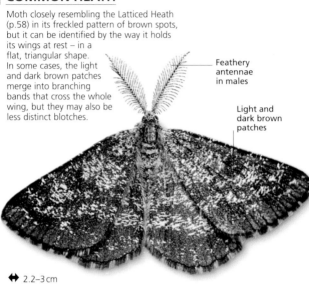

↔ 2.2–3 cm

## DINGY SKIPPER

Butterfly that looks more like a drab moth than a skipper. While perching, it holds its wings out wide so both forewings and hindwings are visible. The forewings have jagged bands of light and dark brown. The hindwings are brown, with a hint of spots along the margin.

Pale and dark bands on forewing

↔ 2.7–3.4 cm

Brown hindwing

»

## LULWORTH SKIPPER

Similar to the Essex Skipper (p.56) and Small Skipper (opposite), but can be told apart by the three or four pale spots on its upperside. These spots are more numerous in the female and resemble a paw print (male shown here). It is found across Europe, but in Britain it is restricted to southern England, around the coastal town of Lulworth, Dorset.

Suffusion of orange-brown

Olive-brown ground colour

↔ 2.4–2.8 cm

## CHEQUERED SKIPPER

Butterfly that holds its forewings – longer and more rounded than those of other skippers – in front of its hindwings. It has many large yellowish markings on its upperside, which contrast with the dark brown background. A similar pattern is seen on the underside, with cream-coloured spots ringed in brown on a pale brown background. It is extinct in England but flourishes in parts of Scotland.

Dark brown ground colour

Yellowish spots

↔ 2.9–3.1 cm

## SMALL SKIPPER

Butterfly best identified by the orange-brown
clubs at the ends of its thick antennae. It is
very similar to, and around the same size as,
the Essex Skipper
(p.56). Both sexes
have a black margin
around the wings, but
only the male (shown here)
has a narrow stripe running
down the wing, parallel to
the leading edge.

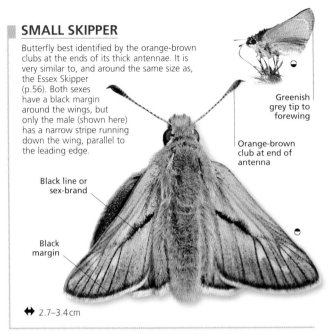

Greenish
grey tip to
forewing

Orange-brown
club at end of
antenna

Black line or
sex-brand

Black
margin

↔ 2.7–3.4 cm

## SILVER-SPOTTED SKIPPER

Butterfly that, like other skippers, holds its wings
diagonally, showing off both the upper and undersides.
It has silver spots on the underside of its hindwings
and yellow spots
on the upperside
of its forewings.

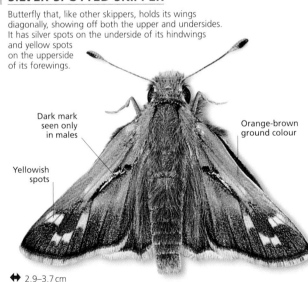

Dark mark
seen only
in males

Orange-brown
ground colour

Yellowish
spots

↔ 2.9–3.7 cm

»

## SHADED BROAD-BAR

Widely distributed moth, with striped appearance
and variable shading. Its wide, triangular wings give
the Shaded Broad-bar the appearance of a wedge
of hardwood, with its many stripes looking like the
grain of a log. This moth flies at night and spends
the day perched on low plants.

Light and dark
brown stripes

Black mark
near wing tip

↔ 2.5–3 cm

## ESSEX SKIPPER

Hairy, orange-brown butterfly, seen
in summer making short, fast flights
between grasses. The forewings
are held at an angle above the
flat hindwings. Both sexes have
black margins to their wings, and
the male has a dark stripe running
down the middle of its forewing
(female shown here). This species is
differentiated from the Small Skipper
(p.55) by the black tips of its
clubbed antennae.

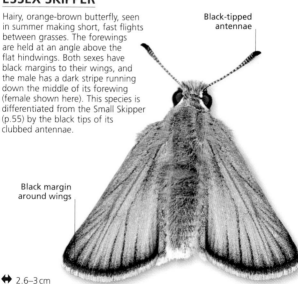

Black-tipped
antennae

Black margin
around wings

↔ 2.6–3 cm

# NORTHERN BROWN ARGUS

Small butterfly found in colder regions and upland areas. It may be distinguished from the more widespread Brown Argus (below) by the fainter orange spots on its brown wings. These spots may not appear at all in some instances.

Dark brown ground colour

Row of faint orange spots near margin

↔ 2.5–3.1 cm

# BROWN ARGUS

Butterfly seen in chalky grasslands from May to September. It has a rich brown upperside – like that of the female Common Blue (p.102) but without a hint of blue. Its paler, almost silver, underside has orange blotches surrounded by black spots.

White streak

Orange spots around margin

↔ 2.5–3.1 cm

White fringe

»

## LATTICED HEATH

Unlike most heaths, which are butterflies, this is a spindly moth. It is named after the tight, net-like brown lines that crisscross the paler wing background. At rest, this moth holds its sail-shaped wings upright, high above the body. It is seen throughout summer on heathland, grassland, and waste ground.

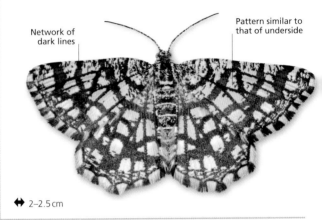

Network of dark lines

Pattern similar to that of underside

↔ 2–2.5 cm

## BURNET COMPANION

Moth found on low plants in sunny grasslands and embankments, sharing its habitat with burnet moths and Mother Shipton (p.62). At rest, its striped forewings are held out wide, with the pale orange stripes of the hindwings visible in between.

Dark brown forewing

Pale orange stripes

↔ 2.5–3 cm

## TRUE LOVER'S KNOT

Moth with delicate black and white spots and stripes on its red-brown wings. At rest, the crossed forewings cover the hindwings entirely, and the rusty tones in the coloration allow the moth to stay hidden when perching on heather, its preferred feeding plant. The True Lover's Knot is seen on moorland and heathland in June and August.

Slightly toothed antennae in males

Red-brown forewing

White spot on forewing

Zigzag white stripes

↔ 2.5–3 cm

## ANTLER

Day-flying moth named after the pale branching pattern – resembling a deer's antlers – on its brown forewings. Males (shown here) are smaller than the females and have feathery antennae. Seen from June to September, this moth feeds on thistles and ragworts.

Black streaks occasionally present on forewing

Feathery antennae

Pale fringes on hindwing

↔ 2.7–3.9 cm

»

## RUBY TIGER

Day- and night-flying moth seen between
April and September. The long, russet-brown
forewings are seen when the moth rests.
The pinkish hindwings have black markings.

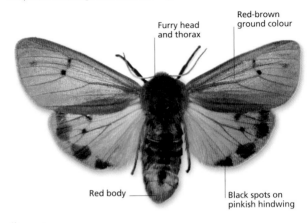

Furry head
and thorax

Red-brown
ground colour

Red body

Black spots on
pinkish hindwing

✦ 3–3.5 cm

## LARGE SKIPPER

Small, hairy butterfly seen basking on large leaves.
It holds its wings out at an angle. The triangular
forewings are orange-brown with orange spots on
the upperside, while the more rounded hindwings
are darker. The underside has a greenish hue.

Dark veins

Orange
spots

Broad, dark
border to
hindwing

✦ 2.9–3.6 cm

## SMALL HEATH

Butterfly that holds its wings upright when resting, with its rounded forewings held high above the hindwings. On the underside, the forewings have an eyespot near the tip, while the darker hindwings have a jagged creamy band running through them. The upperside, only seen in flight, is plain and uniformly coloured.

Narrow brown margin

Orange-brown ground colour

↔ 3.3–3.7 cm

## MUSLIN MOTH

Spring-flying moth seen in a wide range of habitats, from sand dunes to hedgerows. It belongs to the ermine moth family. Like other ermine moths, it has a hairy crest on its back. The male (shown here) is brown, while the female is grey-white, with black speckles on almost transparent wings.

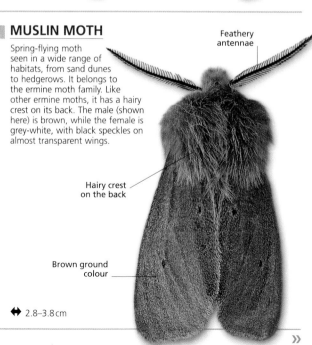

Feathery antennae

Hairy crest on the back

Brown ground colour

↔ 2.8–3.8 cm

»

## MOTHER SHIPTON

Moth named after a
16th-century English witch
for the large brown blotch on
each forewing, said to resemble
a side view of her face, with a
rather large nose. Common on
grassland, downland, and waste
ground, it looks like a butterfly,
flying short distances between
flowers. It rests with its wings
held flat, the white-spotted
hindwings partially visible.

Complex light
and dark pattern

Marking
resembles
witch's chin

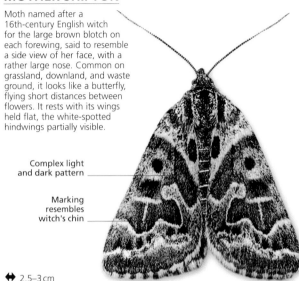

✦ 2.5–3 cm

## BROWN SILVER-LINE

Evening- and night-flying moth, with two
horizontal, silvery lines running across the
triangular forewings, which range from
straw to pale brown. Common in
early summer, it is easily disturbed
from heathland ferns and
woodland shrubs where
it rests by day. It is also
frequently attracted
by lights.

Pale brown
forewing

Silvery
white
cross-line

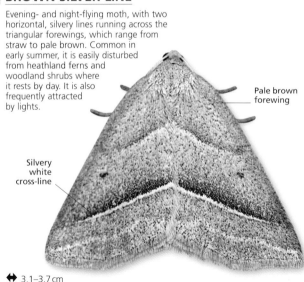

✦ 3.1–3.7 cm

## DUSKY SALLOW

Mottled, pale brown moth, frequently found feeding on knapweed and ragwort. A grassland moth, it is commonly found in chalk and shingle areas, where its straw-coloured wings provide camouflage against the pale soils. It is seen in late summer and autumn.

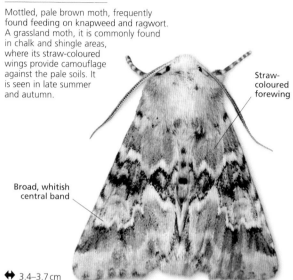

Straw-coloured forewing

Broad, whitish central band

↔ 3.4–3.7 cm

## MOUNTAIN RINGLET

Butterfly with remarkably similar upper and undersides. Both have a brown ground colour, with a band of black spots on a strip of orange that runs along the trailing edges of the wings. Seen in summer only, the Mountain Ringlet is adapted to life at high-altitude habitats, such as moorlands and short grasslands.

Brown ground colour

Orange band

Variable number of black spots

↔ 3.2–4.2 cm

»

# Senses

**Butterflies and moths deploy complex sensory organs in their search for mates and the sugary foods needed to power their flight.**

To find what they need, butterflies and moths use the same set of senses as other animals, including humans. However, their sense organs are different from ours and give them a different perception of the world. These sense organs are adapted to suit their specific requirements of mating and feeding.

## Sight

Caterpillars have simple eyes, capable of little more than telling light from dark. However, adult butterflies and moths have large compound eyes, where thousands of individual lenses work together to produce an overall image. These eyes do not give a very detailed view, but they are very sensitive to motion and colour.

**Rounded compound eye gives a wide field of view**

**Different colours**
Unlike humans, butterflies and moths can detect ultraviolet (UV) light. Flowers look different in UV light (right, bottom) – with the nectar and pollen distinctly visible – than they would in visible light (right, top).

## Smell

Like other insects, moths and butterflies detect smells with their antennae. This is especially important for night-flying moths, helping them find food in the dark and locate mates. Male moths are among those with the best sense of smell in the animal kingdom, as they need to detect the pheromones produced by their female mates.

**Feathery shape helps collect odours from air**

**EMPEROR MOTH**

## Taste

Butterflies and moths do not taste with their mouthparts. They have taste receptors on their feet, so just landing on a flower will tell them whether it is good to sip nectar from.

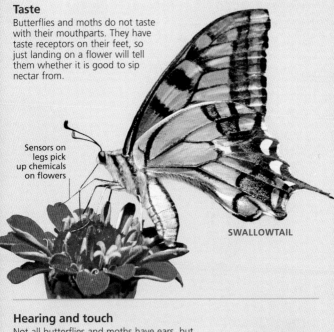

Sensors on legs pick up chemicals on flowers

SWALLOWTAIL

## Hearing and touch

Not all butterflies and moths have ears, but they can "hear" loud noises as the sound waves collide with the scales on the wing surface. Some species have ear-like sensors on the wing to pick up specific sounds of predators. Hair-like scales, or setae, on the body can detect air currents in flight.

Scales on wings help pick up sounds

SETAE COVERING THE BODY

HIGH BROWN FRITILLARY

## WHITE-LETTER HAIRSTREAK

Rarely seen butterfly that lives high in the branches of elm trees, seldom coming to ground level. It has a white line along the underside, which forms the letter W on the hindwings. Each hindwing also has two small tail streamers.

W-shaped marking

Dark brown ground colour

↔ 2.5–3.5 cm

Faint orange spot

## LIGHT ORANGE UNDERWING

Moth with mottled brown forewings that help camouflage it on bark. When resting, the moth's forewings cover the hindwings, which have wide zigzag markings of orange and black. These markings are visible when it is in flight. This moth is seen in aspen forests in spring.

Mottled brown forewing

Orange markings on hindwing

↔ 3.5 cm

# BLACK HAIRSTREAK

Butterfly with broken white stripes curving across its underside. The underside also has a crescent of orange along the margin of the hindwings, accompanied by a series of small black ovals. The upperside is uniformly brown, with faint orange markings along the wing edges.

White stripe

Faint orange marking

↔ 3.5–4 cm    Tail streamer

# BORDERED STRAW

Moth named after the pale brown hue of its wings. The Bordered Straw has darker triangular marks butting up to the leading edges of its forewings. It is one of the few moths to be seen across Europe throughout the year, but it is most common during summer.

Very slender antennae

Pale brown wing

Dark brown spot on edge of forewing

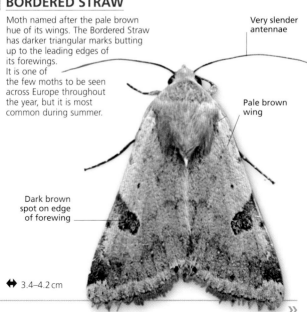

↔ 3.4–4.2 cm

»

## VAPOURER

Distinctive orange-brown moth with a bell-like wing shape. Female Vapourers do not metamorphose into winged adults but remain in caterpillar form. Male Vapourers (shown here) fly through the autumn and have feathery antennae to sniff out mates.

White spot
on forewing

↔ 2.5–3 cm

Red-brown
ground colour

## CHALKHILL BLUE (FEMALE)

Female butterfly with a dark brown upperside, unlike the sky blue male of its species (p.102). The underside is silver-grey with brown spots in white rings. This butterfly flies from July to September in habitats with chalky soils.

Dark brown
ground colour

Orange
spots
along
margin

↔ 3.3–4 cm

Chequered
fringe

# BORDERED WHITE

Moth that holds its triangular brown wings upright while at rest, looking like a drab butterfly. It flies during the day and night in early summer and is common in conifer forests. The wings have a broken white band running away from the body. Females have an orange tinge, while males (shown here) are yellower.

Feathered antennae

White bands on wings

↔ 3.5–4 cm

# GRASS WAVE

Small, striped moth seen in early summer on dry days. The rest of the time, the Grass Wave rests on low-level foliage. As with most moths, it rests with the wings held flat. It has four brown stripes on the forewing and three on the hindwing, which often remains hidden.

Feathered antennae

Pale grey-brown ground colour

↔ 3.6–4.1 cm

»

## BROWN HAIRSTREAK

Butterfly with a streak of white on the underside of both its wings. The more brightly coloured female has a brown upperside, with orange blocks on its forewings. These blocks are paler and fragmented in males.

Orange-brown ground colour

Conspicuous orange patch

Tail streamer on hindwing

♀

Pale orange patch

♂

↔ 3.6–4.5 cm

Uniform dark brown wings

## LARGE HEATH

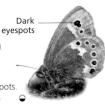

Dark eyespots

Butterfly normally seen with wings closed, displaying its oak brown to grey underside with a grey margin. The chestnut upperside is only glimpsed when the butterfly flies. Its brown forewing may have faint eyespots, while the hindwing often bears a row of spots. It can be found in boggy areas from June to August.

Orange-buff ground colour

Faint eyespot

↔ 3.5–4 cm

## SCOTCH ARGUS

Broad lilac-grey band

Slow-flying butterfly seen in highland areas. Its upperside has a ribbon of eyespots on an orange band along the wing margin. The more marbled underside has an orange band on the forewing, which changes to grey on the hindwing.

Eyespots with highlights

↔ 4.4–5.2 cm

»

# RINGLET

Brown butterfly with several distinctive yellow and black eyespots on each wing. These are most obvious on the underside and sometimes absent from the upperside. Seen on wild flowers in summer, it has a pale fringe to its wings on both sides.

White highlights

↔ 4.2–5.2 cm

Dark, sooty brown ground colour

Two faint eyespots on each wing

# WALL BROWN

Butterfly named after the way it basks on walls, rocks, and bare ground. At rest, the Wall Brown holds its wings upright, displaying its mottled, brown and grey underside with a single eyespot on the forewing. Its orange upperside also bears this eyespot.

Brown banding

Eyespot on forewing

Grey-brown marbled hindwing

↔ 4.5–5.3 cm

# GYPSY MOTH

Large moth often seen perching on trunks of deciduous trees in late summer. The females are pale cream with dark wavy lines and do not fly at all. Male Gypsy Moths (shown here) have wavy bands of brown and feathery antennae. This moth is rare, seen only at a few sites in southern England.

Strongly feathered antennae

Pale, thin wing margin

✥ 3.2–5.5 cm

# SPECKLED WOOD

Butterfly with a browner northern form than its orange-brown southern variety. On the upperside, a single eyespot appears near the tip of the forewing, with up to three more at the margin of the hindwing. Only the forewing eyespot is clearly visible on the marbled underside.

Pale spots on hindwing

Orange and brown ground colour

✥ 4.6–5.6 cm

»

## GRAYLING

Sun-loving butterfly, seen perching with closed wings held above the body, hiding much of the forewing underside beneath its hindwing. The mottled brown pattern of its hindwing underside makes it hard to spot against tree trunks. The tip of the male's forewing, on the underside, is a brighter orange-brown than that of the female (male shown here).

Irregular whitish band

Pale eyespots on forewing

◆ 5 cm

Variable buff-orange markings

## MEADOW BROWN

Butterfly with a distinctive black eyespot near the tip of the forewing. The males have a dark grey-brown upperside and a grey underside. The females (shown here) are more orange-brown on both sides of the wing. Meadow Browns can be seen in large numbers in meadows, hedgerows, and woodland edges.

Single white dot inside eyespot

◆ 5 cm

Brown ground colour

# FOX MOTH

Moth named after the fox-red hues of its brown wings. The females (shown here) are more grey-brown than the males. The forewings have two narrow pale bands, and are longer and more rounded in the females. Fox Moths are seen in early summer on heathland, grassland, and open woodland.

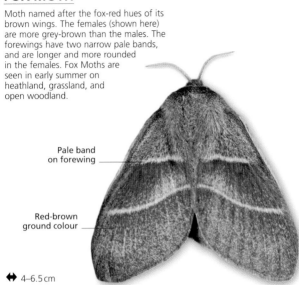

Pale band on forewing

Red-brown ground colour

↔ 4–6.5 cm

# OAK EGGAR

Moth with a pale spot within a russet ring on each forewing. A curving band of cream runs across both wings. This is more obvious in the darker males (shown here) seen zigzagging in the summer sunshine. Females are paler and come out at dusk. This moth is also known as the Northern Eggar.

Light band on wings

Feathery antennae

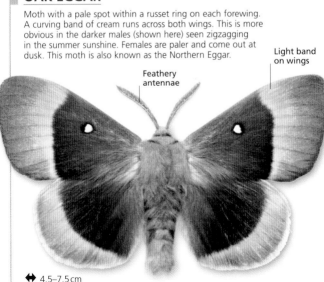

↔ 4.5–7.5 cm

# 6 GREY BUTTERFLIES AND MOTHS

Although some butterflies do have grey markings, it is never their main colour. However, many moths are predominantly grey. Moths are more active at night, a time when their grey coloration provides good camouflage.

## GARDEN CARPET

Dusk-flying moth, which can be seen among cabbages and broccoli and basking on walls and fences by day. Unlike other carpets, its triangular wings have a more rounded trailing edge. Its forewings have distinctive dark blotches along the leading edges. This moth is on the wing from April to September.

Pale grey forewing

Dark blotch on forewing

↔ 1.8–2.5 cm

## COMMON CARPET

Moth with alternating bands of dark and pale grey running across its forewings. The first of its three distinct bands begins behind the head, followed by a wide central band, and finally a dark fringe to the trailing edges of the forewings.

Band comprising complex pattern of light and dark stripes

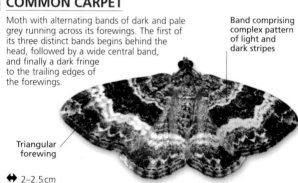

Triangular forewing

↔ 2–2.5 cm

## STRIPED TWIN-SPOT CARPET

Moth with a varied mix of crisscross pale grey or brown lines and darker grey-brown spots. A slightly darker band runs across its forewings, with a dark grey, almost black, spot near each leading edge. It is seen in summer in upland areas.

Dark spot on forewing

Brown ground colour

↔ 2.9–3.1 cm

## LEAD BELLE

Moth with narrow brown stripes across its forewings. Each forewing also has a teardrop-shaped black spot sitting between two stripes. The Lead Belle can be seen around May and June.

Teardrop-shaped black spot

Narrow brown stripe

↔ 3–3.8 cm

## CHALK CARPET

Moth with distinctive triangular forewings – a characteristic of carpet moths. It is found in chalk and limestone areas, its muted grey patterns providing camouflage among pale soils and rocks. A wide band of grey, slightly darker than its ground colour, runs across the back.

Wide grey band

Wide forewing

↔ 3.2–3.8 cm

## SILVER Y

Moth named for white markings resembling the letter Y on its forewings. At rest, the wings are held tent-like over its body. It is seen all year round but is most common in autumn, when it lays its eggs on nettles and clovers.

Robust, hairy body

Greyish brown ground colour

Scalloped hindwing margin

↔ 3.5–4 cm

»

## YELLOW-RINGED CARPET

Moth with triangular grey forewings that have
jagged brown, orange, and yellow bars. These
markings provide camouflage as the moth rests
on lichen-covered rocks in limestone areas. It is
seen in the summer.

Grey
band

Orange
and yellow
marking

Wavy patterns
across wings

✦ 3.4–3.9 cm

## TREBLE-BAR

Dusk-flying moth with three distinctive dark bars running across
its forewings. These bars – made up of fine black and grey lines –
are either curved or angled. The top bar is the smallest and
is often missing. Seen from May to September, the Treble-bar
flies at night. It rests on low foliage by day but may take
off when disturbed.

Wings held
in triangular
position at rest

Dark bar
on forewing

✦ 3.7–4.3 cm

## HUMMINGBIRD HAWK-MOTH

Day-flying moth with pointed wings that beat in a fast, blurry motion. It resembles a hummingbird as it hovers beside tubular flowers, such as fuschia, sipping nectar with its long proboscis. It is seen all year round but mostly in summer. This moth is becoming more common in northern Britain as the climate warms.

Greyish brown forewing

Black and white chequered body

Orange hindwing

↔ 4–5 cm

## EMPEROR MOTH

Night-flying moth, sometimes seen during the day. It has a large eyespot on all four wings and at rest, with its hindwings hidden, it mimics the face of a small mammal. Females are larger and seen more often, while males are generally browner and have leaf-shaped, feathery antennae.

Leaf-shaped antennae

♂

Large furry body

Large eyespot

Greyish ground colour

↔ 4–6 cm

♀

»

# 7 BLACK BUTTERFLIES AND MOTHS

Black is a common colour in butterflies and moths, but it is seldom the dominant one. In many species, black is generally the ground colour of the wings and body, but it is frequently paired with conspicuous white elements.

## CURRANT CLEARWING

Moth with a wasp-like appearance – a black body, transparent wings, and thin yellow bands encircling its abdomen. It has long, narrow forewings and much smaller hindwings. Named after its association with currant plants, this clearwing is often also found near other fruit.

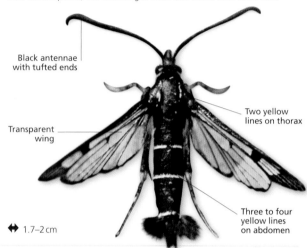

Black antennae with tufted ends

Transparent wing

Two yellow lines on thorax

Three to four yellow lines on abdomen

↔ 1.7–2 cm

## SMALL ARGENT AND SABLE

Black-and-white moth found in damp moorlands and hedgerows throughout summer. It is similar to the Argent and Sable (p.86), but it is a little smaller and closer inspection reveals its bands of black to be broken into blotches.

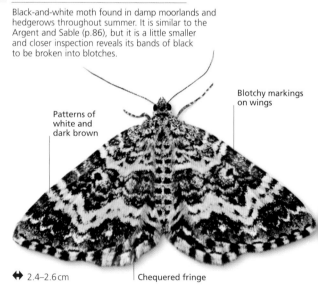

Blotchy markings on wings

Patterns of white and dark brown

↔ 2.4–2.6 cm

Chequered fringe

# CHIMNEY SWEEPER

Sooty black moth seen throughout summer in sunny hay meadows. When newly emerged, the Chimney Sweeper is almost entirely black except for a few faint white markings near the wing tips. As the moth ages, it takes on a brownish hue. These older specimens may be mistaken for female Small Blues (p.51) but for the white fringes on the wing tips.

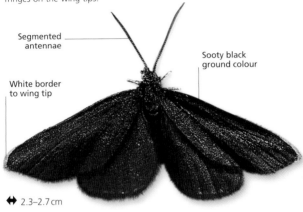

Segmented antennae

Sooty black ground colour

White border to wing tip

↔ 2.3–2.7 cm

# RED-NECKED FOOTMAN

Moth with long, straight black wings. When folded around its body, the wings resemble the cape of a footman. A small portion of the bright red-orange body peeps out at the top of the cape-like wings, resembling a collar. The Red-necked Footman is seen in woodland in early summer.

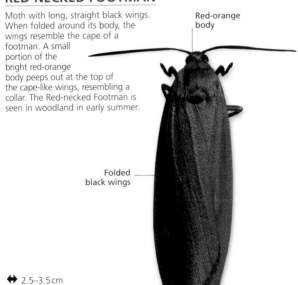

Red-orange body

Folded black wings

↔ 2.5–3.5 cm

»

## ARGENT AND SABLE

Day-flying moth with salt-and-pepper wings. The
black section runs along the wings' trailing edges,
followed by a white band with tiny black spots. Its
wings, triangular at
rest, fold out more
like a butterfly's as
it prepares to fly. It
is seen in early
and midsummer
in damp, marshy
habitats.

Black and white
arcs and blotches
near inner wing

Dark, plump
body with narrow
white stripes

◆ 3.4–3.8 cm

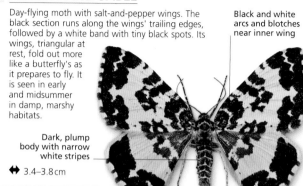

## MAGPIE MOTH

Night-flying moth with white wings covered in
black and orange blotches. This moth can have
anything from a few black spots to a dense
mass of black. The bold patterns on its body
make it look
poisonous to
predators. It is
commonly found
in late summer.

Yellow
S-shaped line

Pale orange
body with
dark spots

◆ 3.5–4 cm

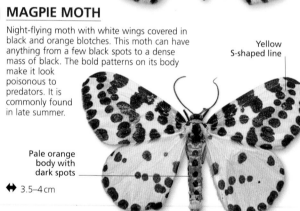

## MAP (SUMMER BROOD)

Butterfly that produces two differently
coloured broods each year – an orange
spring brood (p.40) and a black summer
one. The summer
brood has chunky
white markings on
a black upperside.
The underside in
both broods is lilac,
with white bands.

Chunky white
markings

◆ 2.4–5 cm

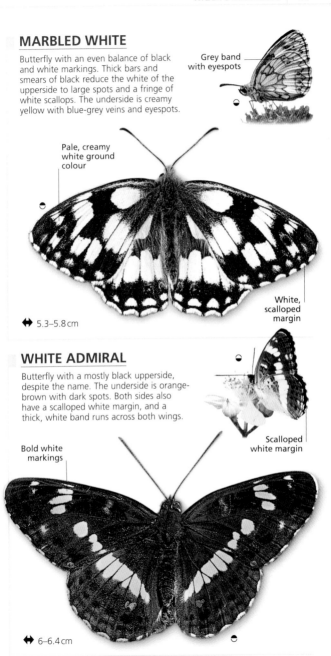

# MARBLED WHITE

Butterfly with an even balance of black and white markings. Thick bars and smears of black reduce the white of the upperside to large spots and a fringe of white scallops. The underside is creamy yellow with blue-grey veins and eyespots.

Grey band with eyespots

Pale, creamy white ground colour

White, scalloped margin

↔ 5.3–5.8 cm

# WHITE ADMIRAL

Butterfly with a mostly black upperside, despite the name. The underside is orange-brown with dark spots. Both sides also have a scalloped white margin, and a thick, white band runs across both wings.

Scalloped white margin

Bold white markings

↔ 6–6.4 cm

# Camouflage and Mimicry

There is a purpose to a butterfly or moth's patterns and colouring. When seen in their natural habitats, it is easy to see why these insects look the way they do.

In nature, bright colours serve as signals, not just to attract mates but also to ward off predators. Moths and butterflies generally keep any bright colours hidden until they need them. What they do put on show is meant to avoid attention, not to attract it.

### Hiding in plain sight

The Comma butterfly finds perfect camouflage among dry foliage, with the underside of its jagged, irregular wings resembling the dried leaves. Commas seen in summer are paler because leaves are not as dry then.

## Camouflage

The primary purpose of the intricate patterns on the wings of most butterflies and moths is to camouflage the insects, so they can rest unseen by predators. Camouflage involves an animal copying the colours of its surroundings and using disruptive patterns, which make it harder to pick out the shape of the entire animal.

### Blending in bark

The grey and brown colouring of the Silver Y moth helps it to stay out of sight when resting on the mottled bark of a tree trunk.

## Mimicry

Some species have patterns that are meant to fool the predator into thinking they are looking at another, more dangerous animal. This phenomenon is called mimicry. Several moths, such as the Hornet Moth, mimic large wasps, and although they cannot sting, other animals stay away from them.

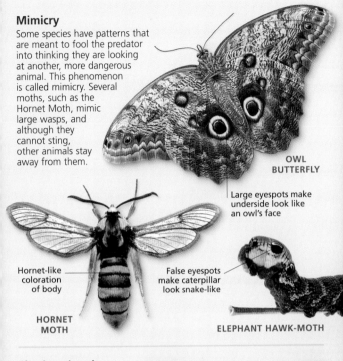

**OWL BUTTERFLY**

Large eyespots make underside look like an owl's face

Hornet-like coloration of body

False eyespots make caterpillar look snake-like

**HORNET MOTH**

**ELEPHANT HAWK-MOTH**

## Sharing signals

The Monarch Butterfly's bright coloration is easy to see and serves as a warning of its toxicity. The Viceroy butterfly is also toxic, and the two species have evolved to look the same – to mimic each other. Working together like this makes the signal more recognizable and effective.

Black line across wing veins

**THE VICEROY**

Dark borders to wings

**MONARCH BUTTERFLY**

# 8 RED BUTTERFLIES AND MOTHS

Some of the most conspicuous and widespread butterflies and moths in Europe – including the Peacock, Painted Lady, and Red Admiral – are shades of red. They range from pink to deep scarlet and maroon, frequently paired with black, blue, and brown markings.

## FIVE-SPOT BURNET

Moth with red spots on shiny black wings. Seen in grasslands in summer, it can be distinguished from its narrow-bordered relative (opposite) by its darker wings and the thick black margins to its hindwings.

Clubbed antennae

Red spots on forewing

Black border of hindwing

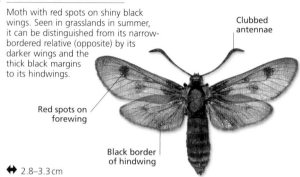

↔ 2.8–3.3 cm

## SIX-SPOT BURNET

Most widespread burnet moth, told apart from related burnets by six red spots on its long forewings. It also has darker wings and a hairier back. Seen throughout summer, it perches on thistles and scabious, or buzzes around slowly on sunny days.

Thick, clubbed antennae

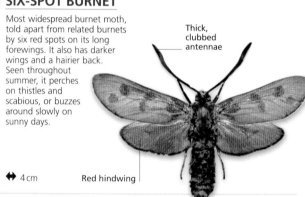

↔ 4 cm          Red hindwing

## CINNABAR

Moth with striking red markings, named after the ore of red mercury. Its forewings are largely charcoal grey, framed with deep red stripes and spots on the trailing edges. The solid red hindwings stand out when the moth holds its wings upright.

Glossy black body

Black hindwing fringe

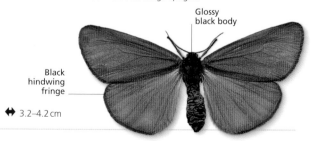

↔ 3.2–4.2 cm

## NARROW-BORDERED FIVE-SPOT BURNET

Burnet moth with black wings and large red spots. It can be told apart from the Five-spot Burnet (opposite) by its longer, more pointed wings, which have a faint blue-green hue. The black band around the hindwings is narrower than that of the Five-spot Burnet.

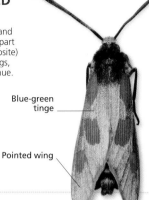

Blue-green tinge

Pointed wing

↔ 3–4.6 cm

## JERSEY TIGER

Moth with black and cream stripes on its triangular forewings. The hindwings may be a conspicuous red or a more muted yellow, with a few black spots. The Jersey Tiger is seen in late summer and early autumn, laying its eggs on nettles.

Unusually angled stripes

Black spot on hindwing

↔ 4.2–5.2 cm

## SCARLET TIGER

Moth with bright red hindwings bearing irregular black patches along the leading and trailing edges. Its hindwings are visible in flight or when flashed to ward off predators. It can be seen in spring in marshy habitats and around river banks.

Forewing pattern extends to thorax

Black forewing with chunky white spots

↔ 4.5–5.5 cm

»

## PEACOCK

Butterfly with bright red upperside and an eyespot of blue, purple, and gold on each wing. The trailing wing edge is jagged, and when held upright, the marbled brown underside looks like a chip of bark. The Peacock can be seen from spring to autumn, frequently in tall grasses.

Jagged wing edge

Reddish maroon ground colour

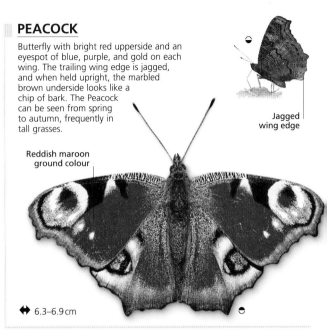

↔ 6.3–6.9 cm

## RED ADMIRAL

Familiar butterfly, frequently seen in flower-filled parks and gardens. The forewings have brown-to-black areas, with white markings near the tips. Brown-red stripes divide these areas from the rest of the brown wings. The underside has a marbled brown pattern, with a pink mark on the forewings.

Smoky brown hindwing

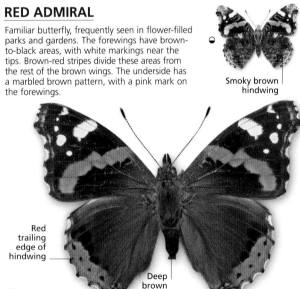

Red trailing edge of hindwing

Deep brown body

↔ 6.2–7.2 cm

# RED UNDERWING

Dusk-flying moth that may also be disturbed from willow or poplar trunks during the day. When it is at rest, its patterned grey forewings hide its red and black hindwings. The distinctive hindwings are only visible in flight or when scaring off attackers. It drinks tree sap and hovers among rotting summer fruit to drink oozing juices.

Red and black banded hindwing

↔ 6.5–7.5 cm

# CAMBERWELL BEAUTY

Widespread, strong-flying butterfly, rare only in the north and west of Europe. A rich maroon covers most of the upperside. The wings have a straw-yellow margin, with a line of blue spots running alongside. Most of the underside is a sooty brown with a jagged white margin.

Rich maroon ground colour

↔ 7.6–8.8 cm

# 9 PURPLE AND BLUE BUTTERFLIES AND MOTHS

Blue and purple – common colours for butterflies – are not always the product of wing pigments. They can be the result of the way light beams interfere with each other as they reflect off the wings.

## SMALL BLUE (MALE)

Butterfly with a blue upperside in the male, unlike the female of the species (p.51), which is dark brown. The male has a subtle blue sheen against the brown ground colour of its upperside and body. The underside in both sexes is pale blue with dark spots ringed in white. Seen throughout summer, it may perch on human skin to feed on sweat.

Dusting of blue near wing base

White fringe

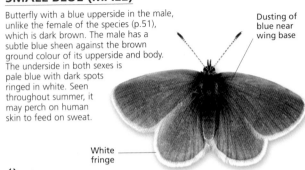

↔ 2–3 cm

## SILVER-STUDDED BLUE

Orange band with black spots

Blue butterfly with a broad white fringe around the wings. The brown upperside has a blue sheen – much more extensive in males (shown here) – that rarely reaches the wing edges. The silver-grey underside is darker in males, and with a margin of orange and blue markings.

Brown margin

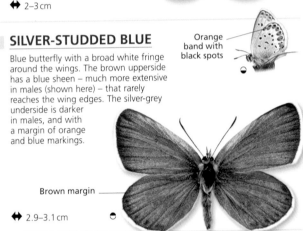

↔ 2.9–3.1 cm

## HOLLY BLUE

White-fringed blue, one of the few that is blue all over. Unlike males (shown here), the females are a paler blue with a wider, smudgy black border to the rounded tip of the forewing. The underside is silver-blue, with a string of small dark spots.

Violet-blue ground colour

Narrow dark margin

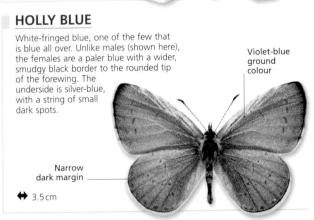

↔ 3.5 cm

## ADONIS BLUE

Butterfly on the wing from May to September. Males (shown here) have a blue upperside with a white margin broken by dark markings. The blue of the female fades to brown around the edges. The malty brown underside has a string of black spots and a row of orange markings near the margin.

Wedge-shaped mark on hindwing

Vibrant blue wing

↔ 3.8 cm

## PURPLE HAIRSTREAK

Butterfly with a white streak on its grey-green underside. The upperside is shiny purple in males. Females (shown here) are brown with purple inner forewings. Mostly seen at rest with wings held upright, it sometimes basks on leaves with its wings held flat.

Orange eyespot at base of hindwing

Sooty brown ground colour

↔ 3.8 cm

## PEA BLUE

Also known as Long-tailed Blue, a brown butterfly with a blue sheen, most apparent in males (shown here). The female's underside is brown with white stripes, while the male's underside is a paler buff. Each hindwing has a long, tassel-like tail.

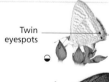

Twin eyespots

Sooty brown ground colour

↔ 3.2–4.2 cm

»

# Migration

While butterflies and moths may not appear to be very strong fliers, some species cover thousands of kilometres every year in epic migrations.

Migration refers to the journey an animal undertakes in search of a better place to feed and reproduce. While migrations are usually round-trips, individual butterflies do not live long enough to make the whole journey. Instead, each brood moves some way along the migration route, and their young will make the next leg.

**Painted Lady**
This butterfly migrates from northern Africa, taking the spring and summer to reach northern Europe. Flying at high altitudes to catch fast winds, it heads back at the start of autumn, covering 14,500 km in total.

EUROPE

AFRICA

**MIGRATION PATH**

### Hummingbird Hawk-moth

This moth migrates into northern Europe in summer but must fly back south in winter to avoid cold weather. One of the fastest Lepidoptera species, it has a top speed of 24 km/h.

**MIGRATION PATH**

EUROPE

### Vagrants

Butterflies blown off their home ranges by strong winds are known as vagrants. Unlike migratory species, these have no way of getting back to their habitats and eventually die out. The Bath White and Camberwell Beauty are common vagrants, blown over to Britain from mainland Europe.

BATH
WHITE

CAMBERWELL
BEAUTY

## COMMON BLUE

Butterfly with orange-brown underside, which can be seen as it feeds with its wings held upright. There are dark spots near the base and orange marks along the back edge of the underside. The male has a violet-blue upperside. This is muted in females, which are browner with orange spots around the edges.

Orange spots

Violet-blue ground colour

Narrow dark margin

♂ ●

Orange spots near margin

Rich brown ground colour

↔ 3.5 cm     ♀ ●

## CHALKHILL BLUE (MALE)

Butterfly with white-fringed wings chequered by brown marks. The pale blue upperside of the male has a solid brown margin, whereas the female's upperside is brown (p.68). Both sexes have a silver-grey underside with brown spots within white rings. This butterfly flies in late summer in chalk and limestone grassland.

Bright sky-blue ground colour

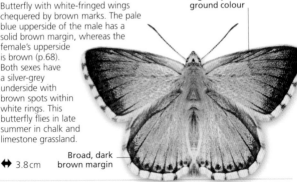

↔ 3.8 cm     Broad, dark brown margin

# LARGE BLUE

Butterfly with a sky-blue upperside and large black spots on the forewings. The trailing edges of both wings have a white fringe and a dark margin, thicker in the females (shown here). The underside is pale blue-grey with numerous black spots ringed in white.

Pale grey-brown ground colour

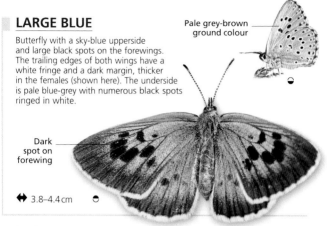

Dark spot on forewing

↔ 3.8–4.4 cm

# PURPLE EMPEROR

Butterfly that appears dull brown but its upperside shimmers with a purple sheen at certain angles in sunlight. A bar of white leads to smaller white spots at the wing tips. Its hindwing has a pair of dark eyespots. The grey-brown underside has an eyespot on the forewing.

Eyespot on forewing

Brown ground colour

Bright purple sheen

↔ 7.5–8.4 cm

White band

# BUTTERFLY GALLERY

This gallery shows the butterfly species profiled in the book, arranged by family. A family is made up of related genera, which in turn are made up of closely related species. Within each family grouping, the butterflies are arranged by colour. Where males and females look substantially different to each other, pictures of both have been included here.

**HESPERIIDAE**
*Skippers*

Grizzled Skipper
*p.51*

Dingy Skipper
*p.53*

Lulworth Skipper
*p.54*

Chequered Skipper
*p.54*

Small Skipper
*p.55*

Silver-spotted Skipper
*p.55*

Essex Skipper
*p.56*

Large Skipper
*p.60*

**PAPILIONIDAE**
*Swallowtails*

Scarce Swallowtail
*p.33*

Swallowtail
*p.33*

**PIERIDAE**
*Yellows and whites*

Orange-tip
*p.19*

Bath White
*p.20*

Green-veined White
*p.20*

Small White
*p.20*

Wood White
*p.21*

Large White
*p.21*

Eastern Dappled White
*p.25*

Brimstone
*p.25*

Pale Clouded Yellow
*p.32*

Clouded Yellow
*p.32*

**LYCAENIDAE**
*Blues, coppers, and hairstreaks*

Green Hairstreak
*p.24*

Duke of Burgundy
*p.36*

»

»

Small Copper
*p.36*

♂ Large Copper
*p.44*

♀ Large Copper
*p.44*

♀ Small Blue
*p.51*

Northern Brown Argus
*p.57*

Brown Argus
*p.57*

White-letter Hairstreak
*p.66*

Black Hairstreak
*p.67*

♀ Chalkhill Blue
*p.68*

♀ Brown Hairstreak
*p.70*

♂ Brown Hairstreak
*p.70*

♀ Common Blue
*p.102*

♂ Small Blue
*p.98*

Silver-studded Blue
*p.98*

Holly Blue
*p.98*

Adonis Blue
*p.99*

Pea Blue
*p.99*

Purple Hairstreak
*p.99*

♂ Common Blue
*p.102*

♂ Chalkhill Blue
*p.102*

Large Blue
*p.103*

**NYMPHALIDAE**
*Fritillaries*

Glanville Fritillary
*p.37*

Gatekeeper
*p.38*

Heath Fritillary
*p.38*

Queen of Spain Fritillary
*p.39*

Small Tortoiseshell
*p.39*

Pearl-bordered
Fritillary
*p.40*

Map (spring brood)
*p.40*

Marsh Fritillary
*p.41*

》

»

Comma
*p.41*

Painted Lady
*p.44*

Silver-washed
Fritillary
*p.45*

High Brown Fritillary
*p.46*

Dark Green Fritillary
*p.46*

Large Tortoiseshell
*p.47*

Monarch
*p.47*

Small Heath
*p.61*

Mountain Ringlet
*p.63*

Large Heath
*p.71*

Scotch Argus
*p.71*

Ringlet
*p.72*

Wall Brown
*p.72*

Speckled Wood
*p.73*

Grayling
*p.74*

**Meadow Brown**
*p.74*

**Map (summer brood)**
*p.86*

**Marbled White**
*p.87*

**White Admiral**
*p.87*

**Peacock**
*p.94*

**Red Admiral**
*p.94*

**Camberwell Beauty**
*p.95*

**Purple Emperor**
*p.103*

# MOTH GALLERY

This gallery profiles the moths included in this book, organized by family and then colour. A family is made up of related genera, which in turn are made up of closely related species. While there are numerous moth families, making up about 90 per cent of Lepidoptera, this book features mostly the day-flying species.

**GEOMETRIDAE**
*Geometer moths*

Blue-bordered Carpet
*p.18*

Silver-ground Carpet
*p.18*

Black-veined Moth
*p.19*

Green Carpet
*p.24*

Barred Yellow
*p.30*

Speckled Yellow
*p.30*

Yellow Shell
*p.30*

The Spinach
*p.31*

Brimstone Moth
*p.31*

Purple-bordered Gold
*p.36*

Orange Underwing
*p.37*

Common Heath
*p.53*

Shaded Broad-bar
*p.56*

Latticed Heath
*p.58*

Brown Silver-line
*p.62*

Light Orange Underwing
*p.66*

Bordered White
*p.69*

Grass Wave
*p.69*

Garden Carpet
*p.78*

Common Carpet
*p.78*

Striped Twin-spot
Carpet
*p.78*

Chalk Carpet
*p.79*

Lead Belle
*p.79*

Yellow-ringed Carpet
*p.80*

Treble-bar
*p.80*

Small Argent and Sable
*p.84*

»

»

Chimney Sweeper
*p.85*

Argent and Sable
*p.86*

Magpie Moth
*p.86*

**LASIOCAMPIDAE**
*Eggars*

Fox Moth
*p.75*

Oak Eggar
*p.75*

**SATURNIIDAE**
*Saturnid moths*

♂
Emperor Moth
*p.81*

♀
Emperor Moth
*p.81*

**SPHINGIDAE**
*Hawk-moths*

Narrow-bordered Bee
Hawk-moth
*p.37*

Hummingbird
Hawk-moth
*p.81*

**NOCTUIDAE**
*Owlet moths*

Beautiful Yellow
Underwing
*p.52*

Field Bindweed Moth
*p.52*

Cloaked Minor
*p.52*

Burnet Companion
*p.58*

True Lover's Knot
*p.59*

Antler
*p.59*

Mother Shipton
*p.62*

Dusky Sallow
*p.63*

Bordered Straw
*p.67*

Silver Y
*p.79*

Red Underwing
*p.95*

**LYMANTRIDAE**
*Tussock moths*

Vapourer
*p.68*

Gypsy Moth
*p.73*

**ARCTIIDAE**
*Tiger moths*

♂ Clouded Buff
*p.31*

♀ Clouded Buff
*p.31*

»

»

Ruby Tiger
*p.60*

Muslin Moth
*p.61*

Red-necked Footman
*p.85*

Cinnabar
*p.92*

Scarlet Tiger
*p.93*

Jersey Tiger
*p.93*

**SESSIIDAE**
*Clearwings*

Hornet Moth
*p.32*

Currant Clearwing
*p.84*

**ZYGAENIDAE**
*Burnets and foresters*

Cistus Forester
*p.24*

Forester
*p.25*

Five-spot Burnet
*p.92*

Six-spot Burnet
*p.92*

Narrow-bordered
Five-spot Burnet
*p.93*

**ENDROMIDAE**
*Kentish Glory*

Kentish Glory
*p.45*

**CRAMBIDAE**
*Grass moths*

Mint Moth
*p.50*

**YPONOMEUTIDAE**
*Ermine moths*

Diamond-back Moth
*p.50*

# Scientific Names

The scientific name of every species consists of two Latin words. The first one is the genus, which is common to closely related species that often look similar. The second is the specific name. The combination of these two words is unique to a particular species.

| Common name | Scientific name | Page |
|---|---|---|
| Blue-bordered Carpet | *Plemyria rubiginata* | 18 |
| Silver-ground Carpet | *Xanthorhoe montanata* | 18 |
| Black-veined Moth | *Siona lineata* | 19 |
| Orange-tip | *Anthocharis cardamines* | 19 |
| Bath White | *Pontia daplidice* | 20 |
| Green-veined White | *Pieris napi* | 20 |
| Small White | *Pieris rapae* | 20 |
| Wood White | *Leptidea sinapis* | 21 |
| Large White | *Pieris brassicae* | 21 |
| Cistus Forester | *Adscita geryon* | 24 |
| Green Hairstreak | *Callophrys rubi* | 24 |
| Green Carpet | *Colostygia pectinataria* | 24 |
| Forester | *Adscita statices* | 25 |
| Eastern Dappled White | *Euchloe ausonia* | 25 |
| Brimstone | *Gonepteryx rhamni* | 25 |
| Barred Yellow | *Cidaria fulvata* | 30 |
| Speckled Yellow | *Pseudopanthera macularia* | 30 |
| Yellow Shell | *Camptogramma bilineata* | 30 |
| The Spinach | *Eulithis mellinata* | 31 |
| Brimstone Moth | *Opisthograptis luteolata* | 31 |
| Clouded Buff | *Diacrisia sannio* | 31 |
| Hornet Moth | *Sesia apiformis* | 32 |
| Pale Clouded Yellow | *Colias hyale* | 32 |
| Clouded Yellow | *Colias croceus* | 32 |
| Scarce Swallowtail | *Iphiclides podalirius* | 33 |
| Swallowtail | *Papilio machaon* | 33 |
| Purple-bordered Gold | *Idaea muricata* | 36 |
| Duke of Burgundy | *Hamearis lucina* | 36 |
| Small Copper | *Lycaena phlaeas* | 36 |
| Orange Underwing | *Archiearis parthenias* | 37 |
| Narrow-bordered Bee Hawk-moth | *Hemaris tityus* | 37 |
| Glanville Fritillary | *Melitaea cinxia* | 37 |
| Gatekeeper | *Pyronia tithonus* | 38 |
| Heath Fritillary | *Melitaea athalia* | 38 |

| | | |
|---|---|---|
| Queen of Spain Fritillary | *Issoria lathonia* | 39 |
| Small Tortoiseshell | *Aglais urticae* | 39 |
| Pearl-bordered Fritillary | *Boloria euphrosyne* | 40 |
| Map (spring brood) | *Araschnia levana* | 40 |
| Marsh Fritillary | *Euphydryas aurinia* | 41 |
| Comma | *Polygonia c-album* | 41 |
| Large Copper | *Lycaena dispar* | 44 |
| Painted Lady | *Vanessa cardui* | 44 |
| Silver-washed Fritillary | *Argynnis paphia* | 45 |
| Kentish Glory | *Endromis versicolora* | 45 |
| High Brown Fritillary | *Argynnis adippe* | 46 |
| Dark Green Fritillary | *Argynnis aglaja* | 46 |
| Large Tortoiseshell | *Nymphalis polychloros* | 47 |
| Monarch | *Danaus plexippus* | 47 |
| Diamond-back Moth | *Plutella xylostella* | 50 |
| Mint Moth | *Pyrausta aurata* | 50 |
| Grizzled Skipper | *Pyrgus malvae* | 51 |
| Small Blue (female) | *Cupido minimus* | 51 |
| Beautiful Yellow Underwing | *Anarta myrtilli* | 52 |
| Field Bindweed Moth | *Tyta luctuosa* | 52 |
| Cloaked Minor | *Mesoligia furuncula* | 52 |
| Common Heath | *Ematurga atomaria* | 53 |
| Dingy Skipper | *Erynnis tages* | 53 |
| Lulworth Skipper | *Thymelicus acteon* | 54 |
| Chequered Skipper | *Carterocephalus palaemon* | 54 |
| Small Skipper | *Thymelicus sylvestris* | 55 |
| Silver-spotted Skipper | *Hesperia comma* | 55 |
| Essex Skipper | *Thymelicus lineola* | 56 |
| Shaded Broad-bar | *Scotopteryx chenopodiata* | 56 |
| Northern Brown Argus | *Aricia artaxerxes* | 57 |
| Brown Argus | *Aricia agestis* | 57 |
| Latticed Heath | *Chiasmia clathrata* | 58 |
| Burnet Companion | *Euclidia glyphica* | 58 |
| True Lover's Knot | *Lycophotia porphyrea* | 59 |
| Antler | *Cerapteryx graminis* | 59 |
| Ruby Tiger | *Phragmatobia fuliginosa* | 60 |
| Large Skipper | *Ochlodes sylvanus* | 60 |
| Small Heath | *Coenonympha pamphilus* | 61 |
| Muslin Moth | *Diaphora mendica* | 61 |
| Mother Shipton | *Callistege mi* | 62 |
| Brown Silver-line | *Petrophora chlorosata* | 62 |

| | | |
|---|---|---|
| Dusky Sallow | *Eremobia ochroleuca* | 63 |
| Mountain Ringlet | *Erebia epiphron* | 63 |
| White-letter Hairstreak | *Satyrium w-album* | 66 |
| Light Orange Underwing | *Archiearis notha* | 66 |
| Black Hairstreak | *Satyrium pruni* | 67 |
| Bordered Straw | *Heliothis peltigera* | 67 |
| Vapourer | *Orgyia antiqua* | 68 |
| Chalkhill Blue (female) | *Polyommatus coridon* | 68 |
| Bordered White | *Bupalus piniaria* | 69 |
| Grass Wave | *Perconia strigillaria* | 69 |
| Brown Hairstreak | *Thecla betulae* | 70 |
| Large Heath | *Coenonympha tullia* | 71 |
| Scotch Argus | *Erebia aethiops* | 71 |
| Ringlet | *Aphantopus hyperantus* | 72 |
| Wall Brown | *Lasiommata megera* | 72 |
| Gypsy Moth | *Lymantria dispar* | 73 |
| Speckled Wood | *Pararge aegeria* | 73 |
| Grayling | *Hipparchia semele* | 74 |
| Meadow Brown | *Maniola jurtina* | 74 |
| Fox Moth | *Macrothylacia rubi* | 75 |
| Oak Eggar | *Lasiocampa quercus* | 75 |
| Garden Carpet | *Xanthorhoe fluctuata* | 78 |
| Common Carpet | *Epirrhoe alternata* | 78 |
| Striped Twin-spot Carpet | *Nebula salicata* | 78 |
| Chalk Carpet | *Scotopteryx bipunctaria* | 79 |
| Lead Belle | *Scotopteryx mucronata* | 79 |
| Silver Y | *Autographa gamma* | 79 |
| Yellow-ringed Carpet | *Entephria flavicinctata* | 80 |
| Treble-bar | *Aplocera plagiata* | 80 |
| Hummingbird Hawk-moth | *Macroglossum stellatarum* | 81 |
| Emperor Moth | *Saturnia pavonia* | 81 |
| Currant Clearwing | *Synanthedon tipuliformis* | 84 |
| Small Argent and Sable | *Epirrhoe tristata* | 84 |
| Chimney Sweeper | *Odezia atrata* | 85 |
| Red-necked Footman | *Atolmis rubricollis* | 85 |
| Argent and Sable | *Rheumaptera hastata* | 86 |
| Magpie Moth | *Abraxas grossulariata* | 86 |
| Map (summer brood) | *Araschnia levana* | 86 |
| Marbled White | *Melanargia galathea* | 87 |
| White Admiral | *Limenitis camilla* | 87 |
| Five-spot Burnet | *Zygaena trifolii* | 92 |

| | | |
|---|---|---|
| Cinnabar | *Tyria jacobaeae* | 92 |
| Six-spot Burnet | *Zygaena filipendulae* | 92 |
| Narrow-bordered Five-spot Burnet | *Zygaena lonicerae* | 93 |
| Scarlet Tiger | *Callimorpha dominula* | 93 |
| Jersey Tiger | *Euplagia quadripunctaria* | 93 |
| Peacock | *Inachis io* | 94 |
| Red Admiral | *Vanessa atalanta* | 94 |
| Red Underwing | *Catocala nupta* | 95 |
| Camberwell Beauty | *Nymphalis antiopa* | 95 |
| Silver-studded Blue | *Plebeius argus* | 98 |
| Holly Blue | *Celastrina argiolus* | 98 |
| Small Blue (male) | *Cupido minimus* | 98 |
| Adonis Blue | *Polyommatus bellargus* | 99 |
| Pea Blue | *Lampides boeticus* | 99 |
| Purple Hairstreak | *Favonius quercus* | 99 |
| Common Blue | *Polyommatus icarus* | 102 |
| Chalkhill Blue (male) | *Polyommatus coridon* | 102 |
| Large Blue | *Phengaris arion* | 103 |
| Purple Emperor | *Apatura iris* | 103 |

# Glossary

Spotting butterflies and moths has its own terminology. There are certain commonly used terms that will help you to understand Lepidoptera better and identify them with greater precision.

**Abdomen** The rear section of a butterfly or moth's body.

**Antennae** A pair of sense organs, also called feelers, located near the front of a butterfly or moth's head.

**Brood** A collection of animals that hatches from a group of eggs laid by the same female or laid at the same time by different females of the same species.

**Camouflage** Body patterns that allow a butterfly or moth to blend in with its surroundings and hide from predators.

**Caterpillar** The larval form of butterflies and moths.

**Chequered** A pattern of squares of alternating colours, often used to refer to the fringe coloration of the wings of a butterfly or moth.

**Chrysalis** The pupal form of a butterfly or moth. In this pupal stage, the larva stops moving and transforms into an adult inside a hard casing, which is referred to as a chrysalis.

**Clubbed** Term used to describe an antenna with a widened tip, appearing club-shaped.

**Cocoon** The protective casing, usually made of silk, within which a pupa transforms into an adult.

**Ermine** A type of white fur; the term is often used to refer to the down (hairs) found on some butterflies and moths.

**Eyespot** A wing marking comprising a colourful spot with concentric circles within, resembling the eye of a mammal or bird.

**Family** A group of related organisms. A family contains several genera (singular: genus), each of which, in turn, contains sets of closely related species.

**Forewing** The front wing of a butterfly or moth.

**Fringe** The area along the edge of a butterfly or moth's wing.

**Fritillary** A type of butterfly, often covered in many dark spots that make its wings look a little like the surface of dice.

**Ground colour** The main background colour of a butterfly or moth's wings.

**Hairstreak** A type of butterfly that has a thin white line, or streak, running along the undersides of its wings.

**Hindwing** The back wing of a butterfly or moth.

**Iridescence** The play of light on certain surfaces, shimmering and changing colour as the angle of view changes.

**Larva** The young, immature form of certain insects, which hatch out of eggs. The larvae of butterflies and moths are generally called caterpillars.

**Leading edge** The front edge of the wing that cuts through the air first as a butterfly or moth flies.

**Marbled** A pattern consisting of differently coloured blotches on a white background, similar to a piece of marble.

**Metamorphosis** The process by which an insect develops from the young form to the adult form. Butterflies and moths undergo complete metamorphosis, via which the wingless young transforms completely to become a winged adult.

**Migrant** An animal that undertakes migration – a long journey, made periodically, to travel to feeding and breeding sites and back.

**Mimicry** A strategy adopted by some butterflies and moths in which they copy the way another animal looks or behaves in an effort to ward off predators.

**Mosaic** A wing patterning made up of many small colourful sections of the same general size.

**Mottled** Having an irregular pattern that is made up of blotches, lines, and smears of varying sizes and often using similar colours.

**Pheromone** A chemical messenger that is released into the air by an animal to attract members of the opposite sex for the purposes of mating. It is detectable by the smell organs of other members of the same species.

**Proboscis** A long, tube-shaped mouthpart used by butterflies and moths to suck up liquids. When not being used, the tube is coiled up under the head.

**Pupa** The middle stage of the life cycle of certain insects, including butterflies and moths, during which the animal becomes relatively inactive while its body transforms from the larval stage to the adult form.

**Scallop** A shape with curved edges – like that of the shell of a scallop, clam, or similar shellfish – seen along the wing margin of some butterflies or moths.

**Scales** Hard plates that cover the body of an animal. A butterfly or moth is covered in scales – flat scales on the wings and hair-like scales on the body.

**Sex-brand** A distinctive patch or line of scent-emitting scales running across the forewing of a male butterfly.

**Setae** Bristles on the body of a butterfly or moth that are used to detect vibrations in the air.

**Skipper** A type of butterfly named after the way it flies – in short flights, or skips.

**Species** A group of related organisms that are able to reproduce with each other.

**Streaked** A pattern consisting of thin lines running through a contrasting colour.

**Streamer** A slender, elongated tail protruding from the trailing edge of the hindwings of some butterflies.

**Tail** A tail-like projection on the trailing edge of the hindwings of some butterfly species.

**Tapered** A term used to refer to a type of moth antenna that is unclubbed and slender.

**Tassel** A narrow structure with a fluffy tip; the term is used to refer to a type of tail found on some butterflies.

**Thorax** The middle section of an insect's body, which lies between the head and the abdomen.

**Trailing edge** The rear edge of the wing that travels through the air behind the rest of the wing.

**Underside** The bottom surface of a wing.

**Upperside** The top surface of a wing.

**Vagrant** An animal that has left its native area and strayed into new areas by accident. Vagrant species generally die out and disappear, but occasionally they do manage to set up home in a new region.

# Index

Butterflies and moths are identified in this index by their common names. A separate list of scientific names of the species in this book can be found on pp.116–19. Page numbers in **bold** indicate main entries.

## A B

Admiral
  Red **94**
  White **87**
Adonis Blue **99**
anatomy 10–11
antennae 11, 64
  clubbed 8
  feathered 9
  hooked 9
  tapered 9
Antler **59**
Argent and Sable 84, **86**
  Small **84**
Argus
  Brown **57**
  Northern Brown **57**
  Scotch **71**
Barred Yellow **30**
Bath White **20**, 101
Beautiful Yellow Underwing **52**
Black Hairstreak **67**
Black-veined Moth **19**
Blue
  Adonis **99**
  Chalkhill (female) **68**
  Chalkhill (male) **102**
  Common 57, **102**
  Holly **98**
  Large **103**
  Pea **99**
  Silver-studded **98**

Blue cont.
  Small (female) **51**
  Small (male) **98**
Blue-bordered Carpet **18**
blues 104–105
body
  abdomen 11
  head 11
  thorax 11, 84
  legs 26, 65
Bordered Straw **67**
Bordered White **69**
Brimstone **25**
Brimstone Moth **31**
brood 13, 40, 86
Brown
  Meadow **74**
  Wall **72**
Brown Argus **57**
Brown Hairstreak **70**
Brown Silver-line **62**
Burnet
  Five-spot **92**
  Narrow-bordered Five-spot **93**
  Six-spot **92**
burnets 114
Burnet Companion **58**

## C

Camberwell Beauty **95**, 101
camouflage 88–89
Carpet
  Blue-bordered **18**
  Chalk **79**
  Common **78**
  Garden **78**
  Green **24**
  Silver-ground **18**
  Striped Twin-spot **78**
  Yellow-ringed **80**
caterpillar 26, 42, 89
Chalk Carpet **79**

Chalkhill Blue
  female **68**
  male **102**
Chequered Skipper **54**
chrysalis 26
Chimney Sweeper **85**
Cinnabar **92**
Cistus Forester **24**
clearwings 114
Cloaked Minor **52**
Clouded Buff **31**
Clouded Yellow **32**
Comma **41**
Common Blue 57, **102**
Common Carpet **78**
Common Heath **53**
compound eyes 64
Copper
  Large **44**
  Small **36**
coppers 105–107
Currant Clearwing **84**

## D E F

Dark Green Fritillary **46**
Diamond-back Moth **50**
Dingy Skipper **53**
distribution 13
Duke of Burgundy **36**
Dusky Sallow **63**
Eastern Dappled White **25**
eggars 112
eggs 26, 27
Elephant Hawk-moth 89
Emperor Moth 13, 64, **81**
Essex Skipper **56**, 54
ermine moths 115
eyes
  compound 64
  simple 64
feeding 42–43
Field Bindweed **52**
Five-spot Burnet **92**

Forester **24**
  Cistus **24**
foresters 114
forewings 10
Fox Moth **75**
Fritillary
  Dark Green **46**
  Glanville **37**
  Heath **38**
  High Brown **46**
  Marsh **41**
  Pearl-bordered **40**
  Queen of Spain **39**
  Silver-washed **45**
fritillaries 107–109

# G H

Garden Carpet 9, **78**
Gatekeeper **38**
geometer moths
  110–13
Glanville Fritillary **37**
grass moths 115
Grass Wave **69**
Grayling **74**
Green Carpet **24**
Green Hairstreak **25**
Green-veined White
  **20**
Grizzled Skipper **51**
Gypsy Moth **73**
habitat 14
Hairstreak
  Black **67**
  Brown **70**
  Green **25**
  Purple **99**
  White-letter **66**
hairstreaks 105–107
Hawk-moth
  Elephant 89
  Hummingbird **81**
  Narrow-bordered
    Bee **37**
hawk-moths 112
hearing 65

Heath
  Common **53**
  Large **71**
  Latticed 53, **58**
  Small **61**
Heath Fritillary **38**
High Brown Fritillary
  **46**, 65
hindwings 10
Holly Blue **98**
Hornet Moth **32**, 89
Hummingbird
    Hawk-moth **81**,
    101

# I J K L

identification 12–13
jagged wing 12
Jersey Tiger **93**
Kentish Glory **45**, 115
Large Blue **103**
Large Copper **44**
Large Heath **71**
Large Skipper **60**
Large Tortoiseshell **47**
Large White **21**
larvae 26
Latticed Heath 53, **58**
Lead Belle **79**
Lepidoptera 10, 101
life cycle 26, 27
Light Orange
    Underwing **66**
Lulworth Skipper 9, **54**

# M

Magpie Moth **86**
Map 13, **40** (spring
    brood), **86**
    (summer brood)
Marbled White **87**
markings
  bands 12
  eyespots 12
  hairstreak 12
  marbling 12

markings *cont.*
  pearls 12
  scallops 12
  spots 12
  veins 12
  wing tips 12
Marsh Fritillary **41**
mating 27
Meadow Brown **74**
metamorphosis 26, 27
migration 100–101
mimicry 88, 89
Mint Moth **50**
Monarch **47**, 89
moth 8–9
Mother Shipton **62**, 68
Mountain Ringlet **63**
mouthparts
  adult 43
  caterpillar 42
Muslin Moth **61**

# N O

Narrow-bordered Bee
    Hawk-moth **37**
Narrow-bordered
    Five-spot Burnet **93**
Northern Brown Argus
    **57**
Oak Eggar **75**
Orange Tip **19**
Orange Underwing **37**
Owl Butterfly 89
owlet moths 112–13

# P

Painted Lady 8, **44**,
    100
Pale Clouded Yellow
    **32**
Pea Blue **99**
Peacock **94**
Pearl-bordered Fritillary
    **40**
pheromones 64
pollen 43

predators
  hiding from 88–89
  detecting 65
proboscis 43
Purple Emperor **103**
Purple Hairstreak **99**
Purple-bordered Gold **36**
pupa 26

# Q R S

Queen of Spain Fritillary **39**
Red Admiral **94**
Red Underwing **95**
Red-necked Footman **85**
reproduction 100, 26–27
Ringlet **72**
  Mountain **63**
Ruby Tiger **60**
saturnid moths 112
scales 11
scallops 12
Scarce Swallowtail **33**
Scarlet Tiger **93**
Scotch Argus **71**
senses 64–65
sensory organs 64
setae 65
sex 13
sex-brand 54
Shaded Broad-bar **56**
sight 64
signal 89
silkworms 43
Silver Y **79**
Silver-ground Carpet **18**
Silver-spotted Skipper **55**
Silver-studded Blue **98**
Silver-washed Fritillary **45**
Six-spot Burnet **92**
Skipper
  Chequered **54**

Skipper *cont.*
  Dingy **53**
  Essex **56**
  Grizzled **51**
  Large **60**
  Lulworth **54**
  Silver-spotted **55**
  Small **55**
skippers 9, 104
Small Argent and Sable **84**
Small Blue
  female **51**
  male 85, **98**
Small Copper **36**
Small Heath **61**
Small Skipper **55**, 56
Small Tortoiseshell **37**, 47
Small White **20**
smell 64
Speckled Wood 13, **73**
Speckled Yellow **30**
Spinach, the **31**
spotting butterflies 14
streamer 12
Striped Twin-spot Carpet **78**
Swallowtail 10, 11, **33**, 65
  Scarce **33**
swallowtails 104

# T U V

tails 12
taste 65
The Spinach **31**
The Viceroy 89
Tiger
  Jersey **93**
  Ruby **61**
  Scarlet **93**
tiger moths 113–14
Tortoiseshell
  Large **47**
  Small **39**

touch 65
toxicity 42, 89
Treble-bar **80**
True Lover's Knot **59**
tussock moths 113
ultraviolet light 64
underside 10
Underwing
  Beautiful Yellow **52**
  Light Orange **66**
  Orange **37**
  Red **95**
upperside 10–11
vagrants 101
Vapourer **68**
veins 12
Viceroy, the **89**
vision 64

# W Y

Wall Brown **72**
White
  Bath **20**
  Bordered **69**
  Eastern Dappled **25**
  Green-veined **20**
  Large **21**
  Marbled **87**
  Small **20**
  Wood **21**
White Admiral **87**
White-letter Hairstreak **66**
whites 105
wings 10
wing pattern 12, 88
Wood White **21**
Yellow 105
  Barred **30**
  Clouded **32**
  Pale Clouded **32**
  Speckled **30**
yellows 105
Yellow Shell **30**
Yellow-ringed Carpet **80**

# Acknowledgments

Dorling Kindersley would like to thank the following people for their assistance in the preparation of this book: Neha Pande and Priyaneet Singh for editorial assistance, Vanya Mittal for design assistance, Steve Setford for proofreading, and Derek Niemann and Claire Thomas at the RSPB.

The publisher would like to thank the following for their kind permission to reproduce their photographs:

(**Key**: a-above; b-below/bottom; c-centre; f-far; l-left; r-right; t-top)

**1 Dorling Kindersley:** Natural History Museum, London (c). **6–7 Dreamstime.com:** Artjazz. **8** Dorling Kindersley: Natural History Museum, London (b). **Dreamstime.com:** Viter8 (cra). **9 Dorling Kindersley:** Paolo Mazzei (tr); Natural History Museum, London (c). **10–11 Dorling Kindersley:** Natural History Museum, London (tc). **11 Dreamstime.com:** Jens Stolt (br). **12 Dorling Kindersley:** Mario Maie (ca); Natural History Museum, London (cla, cra, cl, cr, clb, cb, crb, bl, bc, br). **Fotolia:** Christian Musat (c). **13 Dorling Kindersley:** Ted Benton (crb); Simon Curson (tl, tr). **14 Dorling Kindersley:** Natural History Museum, London (br). **Dreamstime.com:** Artjazz (clb); Hensor (tr); Vladimir Gurov (cl); Colette6 (cr). **Fotolia:** Jenny Thompson (cb). **15 Dreamstime.com:** Jerryway. **16–17 Dreamstime.com:** Manon Ringuette. **18 FLPA:** Richard Becker (b); Gianpiero Ferrari (c). **19 Dorling Kindersley:** Natural History Museum, London (bc). **Dreamstime.com:** Mille19 (cr). **FLPA:** Martin B Withers (t). **20 Dorling Kindersley:** Ted Benton (cra); Natural History Museum, London (tr, tc, bc). **21 Dorling Kindersley:** Natural History Museum, London (tr, tc, b). **22–23 rspb-images.com:** Steve Round. **24 Dorling Kindersley:** Paolo Mazzei (c); Natural History Museum, London (crb). **Fotolia:** hfox (tc). **25 Alamy Images:** Naturepix (b). **Dorling Kindersley:** Ted Benton (cra, crb); Natural History Museum, London (tc). **27 Fotolia:** crystalseye (br). **28–29 Dreamstime.com:** Eric Gevaert. **30 Dorling Kindersley:** Paolo Mazzei (c); Jens Schou (tc). **31 Dorling Kindersley:** Jens Schou (tc). **FLPA:** Ian Rose (crb, bc). **32 Dorling Kindersley:** Natural History Museum, London (tc). **Dreamstime.com:** Jedendva (b). **Fotolia:** Christian Musat (c). **33 Dorling Kindersley:** Natural History Museum, London (t, b). **34–35 Dreamstime.com:** Jens Stolt. **36 Dorling Kindersley:** Natural History Museum, London (c, crb, bc). **FLPA:** Gianpiero Ferrari (tc). **37 Dorling Kindersley:** Mario Maier (bc). **Fotolia:** Gucio_55 (c). **38 Dorling Kindersley:** Ted Benton (c, cr); Paolo Mazzei (tr); Mario Maier (bc). **39 Dorling Kindersley:** Natural History Museum, London (tr, c, cr, b). **40 Dorling Kindersley:** Ted Benton (tr); Mario Maier (cr). **41 Dorling Kindersley:** Ted Benton (tr); Natural History Museum, London (cr, b); Paolo Mazzei: (c). **42 Dreamstime.com:** Torbjörn Swenelius (br). **43 123RF.com:** Sandeep Kharat (tr). **Dreamstime.com:** Dfikar (cl). **44 Dorling Kindersley:** Natural History Museum, London (cla, c). **45 Dreamstime.com:** Jens Stolt (b). **rspb-images.com:** Richard Revels (tr). **47 Dorling Kindersley:** Paolo Mazzei (c); Natural History Museum, London (b). **48–49 Dreamstime.com:** Johannes Mayer. **50 Dreamstime.com:** Darius Baužys (bc). **FLPA:** Nigel Cattlin (tr). **51 Dorling Kindersley:** Natural History Museum, London (tc). **Fotolia:** Cosmin Manci (tc). **52 Alamy Images:** Premaphotos (tc). **FLPA:** Neil Bowman (bc); Gianpiero Ferrari (c). **53 Dorling Kindersley:** Natural History Museum,

London (b). **Fotolia:** M.R. Swadzba (tc). **54 Dorling Kindersley:** Natural History Museum, London (b). **55 Fotolia:** philip kinsey (c). **56 Dreamstime. com:** Christopher Smith (tc). **rspb-images.com:** Richard Revels (bc). **57 Dorling Kindersley:** Natural History Museum, London (cr, bc). **Fotolia:** S.R.Miller (tc). **58 Alamy Images:** Arco Images / Huetter, C. (tc). **Fotolia:** fotofreakdgy (bc). **59 Dorling Kindersley:** Natural History Museum, London (bc). **Chris Gibson:** (tr). **60 Dorling Kindersley:** Natural History Museum, London (tc, bc). **61 Dreamstime.com:** Darius Baužys (br). **62 FLPA:** Gianpiero Ferrari (bc). **63 FLPA:** Richard Becker (t). **64 Dorling Kindersley:** Paolo Mazzei (br). **Science Photo Library:** Cordelia Molloy (cr). **65 Dorling Kindersley:** Mario Maier (b, crb). **Dreamstime.com:** Paleka (tc). **66 Dorling Kindersley:** Natural History Museum, London (tr, c). **FLPA:** Gianpiero Ferrari (bc). **67 Dorling Kindersley:** Ted Benton (tr). **Andy MacKay:** (br). **68 Dorling Kindersley:** Natural History Museum, London (tc). **69 Andy MacKay:** (b). **70 Dorling Kindersley:** Natural History Museum, London (tc). **rspb-images.com:** Richard Revels (bc). **71 Dorling Kindersley:** Mario Maier (tr); Natural History Museum, London (tc). **Dreamstime.com:** Cosmin Manci (b). **72 Dorling Kindersley:** Ted Benton (bc); Natural History Museum, London (tr, tc); Paolo Mazzei (cr). **73 Dorling Kindersley:** Natural History Museum, London (tc, cr, bc). **74 Dorling Kindersley:** Natural History Museum, London (tc). **75 Dorling Kindersley:** Natural History Museum, London (bc). **FLPA:** Nigel Cattlin (cr). **76–77 Dreamstime.com:** Dmitry Zhukov. **78 Dorling Kindersley:** Natural History Museum, London (cra). **Fotolia:** barry1 (c). Chris Gibson: (b). **79 Dorling Kindersley:** Natural History Museum, London (bc). **FLPA:** Gianpiero Ferrari (tc). **Andy MacKay:** (c). **80 Dreamstime.com:** Michael Smith (bc). **Chris Gibson:** (tc). **81 Dorling Kindersley:** Paolo Mazzei (cr); Natural History Museum, London (tc). **82–83 Dreamstime.com:** Michael Smith. **84 FLPA:** Gianpiero Ferrari (bc). Chris Gibson: (tc). **85 Dorling Kindersley:** Paolo Mazzei (c). **Dreamstime.com:** Darius Baužys (bc). **86 Dorling Kindersley:** Natural History Museum, London (tc, c, bc). **87 Dorling Kindersley:** Ted Benton (bc, c); Mario Maier (tr). **88 rspb-images.com:** Tony Hamblin (br); Richard Revels (cl). **89 Dorling Kindersley:** Natural History Museum, London (cl, crb). **Dreamstime.com:** Saskia Massink (cr). **90–91 Dreamstime.com:** Fotofred. **92 Dorling Kindersley:** Natural History Museum, London (c, bc). **Science Photo Library:** F. Martinez Clavel (tc). **93 Dorling Kindersley:** Natural History Museum, London (c, bc). **Dreamstime.com:** Darius Baužys (tr). **94 Dorling Kindersley:** Ted Benton (tr); Natural History Museum, London (cr, bc); Mario Maie (c). **95 Dorling Kindersley:** Paolo Mazzei (c); Natural History Museum, London (bc). **96–97 Dreamstime.com:** Torbjörn Swenelius. **98 Dorling Kindersley:** Natural History Museum, London (cb, bc); Ilaria Pimpinell (cra). **rspb-images.com:** David Kjaer (tr). **99 Dorling Kindersley:** Mario Maier (crb); Natural History Museum, London (tc, cra, cr, br); Ilaria Pimpinelli (tr). **100 FLPA:** Gary K Smith (c). **101 Dorling Kindersley:** Natural History Museum, London (bl, br). **Dreamstime.com:** Dmitriy Goncharenko (c). **102 Dorling Kindersley:** Ted Benton (cla, bc); Natural History Museum, London (cb); Mario Maier (tr). **103 Dorling Kindersley:** Ted Benton (tr); Natural History Museum, London (cr, b); Paolo Mazzei (ca). **104 Dorling Kindersley:** Natural History Museum, London (ca, cra, c, crb, bc, br). **Fotolia:** philip kinsey (cr). **rspb-images.com:** Richard Revels (cb). **105 Alamy Images:** Naturepix (cr). **Dorling Kindersley:** Natural History Museum, London (tc, tr, ca, cra, cl, br).

**Dreamstime.com:** Jedendva (cb). **Fotolia:** Christian Musat (clb). **106 Dorling Kindersley:** Natural History Museum, London (tl, tc, tr, cra, cl, clb, crb, bc, br). **Fotolia:** Cosmin Manci (cla); S.R.Miller (ca). **rspb-images.com:** David Kjaer (bl); Richard Revels (cb). **107 Dorling Kindersley:** Ted Benton (cr, cla, ca); Natural History Museum, London (tl, tc, tr, cb, crb, br); Mario Maier (clb, c); Paolo Mazzei (cra). **108 Dorling Kindersley:** Ted Benton (bl); Natural History Museum, London (tr, cl, clb, crb, bc); Mario Maier (ca); Paolo Mazzei (tl, cra). **Dreamstime.com:** Cosmin Manci (cb). **109 Dorling Kindersley:** Ted Benton (cla); Natural History Museum, London (tl, tc, cra, cl, c); Mario Maie (ca); Mario Maier (tr). **110 Dorling Kindersley:** Paolo Mazzei (c, clb); Jens Schou (cr, crb). **FLPA:** Richard Becker (cra); Gianpiero Ferrari (ca, bc); Martin B Withers (cl). **111 Alamy Images:** Arco Images / Huetter, C. (tr). **Dorling Kindersley:** Natural History Museum, London (c). **Dreamstime.com:** Christopher Smith (tc); Michael Smith (bc). **FLPA:** Gianpiero Ferrari (cla, crb, br). **Fotolia:** barry1 (cr); M.R. Swadzba (tl). **Chris Gibson:** (clb, bl). **Andy MacKay:** (cl, cb). **112 Alamy Images:** Premaphotos (bc). **Dorling Kindersley:** Simon Curson (cr); Natural History Museum, London (tc, tr, cra, clb); Paolo Mazzei (tl, c/Emperor). **FLPA:** Nigel Cattlin (ca); Gianpiero Ferrari (br). **Fotolia:** Gucio_55 (c). **113 Dorling Kindersley:** Paolo Mazzei (cr); Natural History Museum, London (cla, c, cb, crb). **FLPA:** Richard Becker (cra); Ian Rose (br, bc); Neil Bowman (tl). **Fotolia:** fotofreakdgy (tc). **Chris Gibson:** (tr). **Andy MacKay:** (cl). **114 Dorling Kindersley:** Natural History Museum, London (tl, cla, ca, cra, c, crb, bc). **Dreamstime.com:** Darius Baužys (tc, tr, br); Victor Savushkin (bl). **Fotolia:** hfox (cb). **Chris Gibson:** (cr). **115 Dreamstime.com:** Darius Baužys (ca); Jens Stolt (tc). **FLPA:** Nigel Cattlin (c).

**Jacket images: Front: Dreamstime.com:** Roger Meerts crb, Mille19 br, Jens Stolt cra, Lorraine Swanson l; **PunchStock:** Westend61; **Back: Dorling Kindersley:** Natural History Museum, London clb, bl; **Spine: Dreamstime. com:** Lorraine Swanson b.

All other images © Dorling Kindersley
For further information see: **www.dkimages.com**

The RSPB speaks out for birds and wildlife, tackling the problems that threaten our environment. Nature is amazing – help us keep it that way. We belong to BirdLife International, the global partnership of bird conservation organizations.

If you would like to know more about the RSPB, visit the website at **www.rspb.org.uk**
or write to:
**RSPB,** The Lodge, Sandy, Bedfordshire SG19 2DL
Tel. 01767 680551